TALKING TOPICS

Gaynor Ramsey   Virginia LoCastro

Contents

To the Teacher

Communication starts with sharing things about ourselves and others. *Talking Topics* is designed to encourage pre-intermediate students to become involved in conversations—in pairs, small groups or as a class—about topics that are within their own personal experience, or awaken their curiosity and interest. *Talking Topics* emphasizes the integration of listening and speaking: the listening passages provide input on the various topics, broadening and deepening the students' background knowledge and experiences.

There are fourteen units in the book, each one covering a different topic. The topics are treated from a variety of angles and the students are always asked to relate the ideas to themselves, their surroundings, their everyday lives, and their pasts. The tasks in each unit can be used individually and in a different order if necessary. Every teacher and every class can determine the content of the lesson, according to the time available and the interests of the students, by selecting the work they want to do.

The first part of each unit serves as an introduction to the topic, very often leading in with picture stimuli or a questionnaire. Each unit also has two listening passages related to the topic of the unit. There is a pre-listening task that students do before listening to the cassette. Here the teacher may need to take an active role in helping the students anticipate and predict the content of the listening. The pre-listening is followed by one or more tasks to be done along with the cassette.

The section called *You and Me* sets up a wide variety of pairwork activities. These activities range from role plays and interviews to word association games and information gap tasks. The students should be given the opportunity to explore the topics together without too much guidance or intervention from the teacher. In some cases, the students are asked to report back on what they found out during this pairwork phase, and in other cases the results can be left as something known only to the two people involved. The teacher will be able to decide what is best for his/her particular students. The section called *Class Talk*, usually at the end of a unit, brings the students back into their class group to consider the topic together.

What sort of preparation needs to be done with the students for these activities?

The sort of preparation, and the time needed to do it, depends mainly on two things:

a) the students' familiarity with the vocabulary and the structures they will have to use

b) the students' experience of activities which emphasize fluency rather than accuracy, and which depend on their active participation to succeed.

If the teacher realizes that necessary vocabularly is not known, then this should be pre-taught, using, wherever possible, the techniques of letting the students ask for vocabulary items that they think they will need. It may be useful to focus students' attention on the structures they will need to use and this is very often done in the units in the form of examples. The *You and Me* sections may require more preparation, particularly in the units where they contain role plays or interviews. The task of carrying out a role play or an interview can seem rather daunting, but the task can be made much more approachable if the teacher carries out a sample role play or a sample interview in the class, so that the students can hear how the questions should be formed.

How do the students actually work on the activities?

Nearly all of the activities and conversations can be carried out in pairs or in small groups. If students are unused to working like this then it might take a short time for them to get used to it. They will probably very soon discover that they are able to say more and become more interested in their fellow learners by working in this way, and will learn to expect that concentrated focus on aspects of language apart from fluency takes place in another lesson or phase. Ideally, the teacher should develop a fast and effective way of dividing the class so that students work with different partners and groups as often as possible. The teacher should also often try to be a member of a group, in such a way as not to inhibit the students' interaction.

What is in the units?

There is a table of contents on page 2. This table gives the following information:

a) the general topic of each unit
b) the lexical areas that are treated, giving an idea of the angles from which the topic is presented
c) the language that is actively practiced—the item in bold print shows the main tense form that is used throughout the unit, the others are language items which occur in one or more tasks in the unit.

What sort of tasks and activities occur throughout the book?

There are some exercise types which can be found throughout the material. These are mainly identifiable by their titles. Here is a list of activity types most often used:

a) *Pictures to Talk About:* this can be found at the beginning of some units and serves to introduce the topic and focus on necessary vocabulary (examples: Unit 1, Part 1; Unit 3, Part 1).
b) *Listening:* the listening tasks usually come in the second and fifth parts of each unit. They aim at providing the students with rich and varied input, slightly above their speaking or writing ability level, enabling them to do the tasks in other parts of the unit more effectively. They also expose the students to additional vocabulary and information on the topic. The tasks are designed so that the students listen first for the gist, then for details in the second or third tasks. The emphasis is on teaching global, integrated listening skills, not testing.
c) *Class Talk:* This aims at bringing the students back together after working in pairs or in groups. The teacher may, however, decide to let the students discuss some of these ideas in smaller groups rather than with the class all together, particularly if the class is large.
d) *Vocabulary:* the puzzle-like activities can be done individually or in groups.
e) *Questionnaire:* this is intended as an introduction to topics, encouraging the students to share their experience first, before going on to aspects that they might have to speculate about (examples: Unit 2, Part 1; Unit 10, Part 1).

f) *You and Me:* these activities can be found in every unit. The pages have been designed so that partner A cannot see what partner B has in his/her book (and vice versa). In addition to role plays and interviews, real information gap tasks are set up. In some cases the students are expected to report back on what they have talked about.

The success of the conversations and activities prompted by the contents of *Talking Topics* depends on a few other factors, apart from the interest level of the students in the topics. The students:

a) should be encouraged to obtain the vocabulary they need in order to say what they want

b) should be made responsible for the actual carrying out of the conversations, tasks, etc.

c) should be able to work in an atmosphere which allows them to become personally involved in what they are saying, and to consider the topics subjectively

d) should work with each other (and with the teacher as one of a group) as often as possible

e) should not be inhibited by correction during an activity (unless a serious misunderstanding has taken place because of incorrect language use).

Happy talking and listening to anyone who uses *Talking Topics*—may your conversations be lively, demanding, and interesting!

To the Student

In *Talking Topics* you can find a lot of things to talk about. You can find a lot of help and ideas, too. If you need more help (with language) or more ideas, ask your teacher. Try to say as much as you can about the topics, and try to let other students get to know you better—people are usually interested in other people! Happy talking! Happy listening!

unit 1 SHOPPING

PART 1 *Pictures to talk about*

A Where are the people in each of these pictures? Write A, B, C, and D here:

1 .... a record store 2 .... a department store
3 .... a supermarket 4 .... a market

A

B

C

D

What are the differences between these places? What do you think the people are buying? What else do you think they can buy here?

B Choose two of the pictures and write two questions that the customers might ask.

Useful language:
Can I...? Do you...?
How much...?

Picture .... 1 ....

2 ....

Picture .... 1 ....

2 ....

Form groups of three or four. Exchange the questions you have in your group. Give possible answers to all the questions.

PART 2 *L i s t e n i n g*

Annette is a student, but she also works part-time in a bakery. She is being interviewed about her job. What kinds of work do you think she does at the bakery? What might be some good and bad points about her job?

A Which is the best summary of the conversation?

1 Annette's job is to put the bread, rolls, and cakes on the shelves in the store. She doesn't enjoy her job very much.

2 Annette's job is to put the bread, rolls, and cakes on the shelves in the store. Sometimes she is also the cashier. She enjoys her job very much.

B Listen again and fill in the chart below.

Kinds of work	Good/bad points	Days	Hours	Pay

Does Annette like her job? Why/Why not?

Interview

A You want to interview the two people below about their jobs for an article in a magazine. Write five questions with *do* or *does* that you plan to ask. Here are some example questions for a man who owns a small delicatessen:

—*How many days a week do you work?*
—*Do you employ anybody to help you in the store?*
—*Does the store open at the same time every day?*
—*Where do you buy your cheese?*
—*What do you like best about your job?*

a young woman who works in a boutique

a store detective in a large department store

B Work with a partner. Your partner is now the store detective or the young woman who works in a boutique. Ask the questions. Make a note of the answers so that you have the information for your article.

C Now write your short article.

PART 4 *Listening*

Some people like to go shopping, but some hate to. How about you? Ask three other people and try to find out why.

Now listen to this conversation about shopping.

A Say whether the following statements are true or false.

1 Donna has been invited to a party.
2 They are talking about shopping for clothes for the party.
3 Shopping is something they both like to do.
4 They decide to go shopping together.

B Check (✓) the reasons for not liking to go shopping.

☐ stores too crowded

☐ unexciting clothes

☐ impolite clerks

☐ impossible to find something one likes

☐ clothes too expensive

C Choose the best synonyms.

1 I really don't know where to look.
to go shopping in general / to find boutiques / to buy good clothes for me
2 But you want to look good for the party.
sweet / attractive / polite
3 I'd really appreciate that.
your attention / your talking with me / your helping me

PART 5   *Y o u   a n d   M e*

Partner A: see page 64.   Partner B: see page 73.

PART 6   *C l a s s   T a l k*

Now make a class report on your Partner A/Partner B interviews.

A: Tell the others about your partner's answers to d) and e).

B: Tell the others about your partner's answers to 2) and 3).

Collect the information on the blackboard like this:

He/she likes buying	He/she hates buying	He/she would enjoy working in	He/she would hate working in

Are there any answers that are the same?

unit 2 S P O R T S

Q u e s t i o n n a i r e

A This is a questionnaire about sports. Ask questions beginning with *Can you. . .?* to five people. Write down what they say like this:

** = yes, pretty well
* = yes, but not very well
X = no

If there is a sport that is very popular in your country and isn't in the questionnaire, write it in as question 10.

NAME					
1 ride a bicycle					
2 play baseball					
3 play tennis					
4 play table tennis					
5 swim					
6 ski					
7 play volleyball					
8 play golf					
9 play badminton					
10					

B Write short reports about three of the sports in the questionnaire. Write about:

1 The sport with the most positive answers
2 The sport with the most negative answers
3 The sport you like best

Example: tennis
Three out of the five people can play tennis. Two can play well and one can play, but not very well.

Example: volleyball
None of the five people can play volleyball well.

L i s t e n i n g

People do sports for many reasons.
For example:

—to keep in shape
—to make friends

Work with a small group and think of some other reasons.

Now listen to this young man talking about the sports he likes.

A Say whether the following statements are true or false.

1 This young man has always liked dangerous activities.
2 At college he's now doing a safer sport.
3 He saw hang-gliding in California.
4 He's never gotten hurt.
5 He wants to try mountain climbing in the future.

B Put a check (✓) next to the sports that are mentioned.

☐ skiing   ☐ ski jumping   ☐ soccer ☐ football

☐ skydiving   ☐ hang-gliding   ☐ baseball

C Write the names of the dangerous activities in the columns.

Past	Present	Future

PART 3 *C l a s s   T a l k*

Which sports do you think are:
—very exciting to watch?
—very boring to watch?
—very dangerous to play?
—very fast to play?

—very slow to play?
—very interesting to watch?
—very good for people who want to
  keep in shape?

Vocabulary

A Which words go with which sports? Choose words from the box and write them under the pictures.

| ball | ball | ball | shuttlecock | club | racket | racket | bat | hole | net | net |

on a badminton court

on a baseball field

on a golf course

on a tennis court

....

....

....

....

....

....

....

....

....

....

....

B You need a ball and a club to play this sport, and you have to hit the ball into a hole with the club. Which sport is this? It's ....

C Write a short description like this about one of the other sports. Read your description to someone and ask them to write down the name of the sport.

PART 5 *Listening*

What sport do you know well? Could you explain the sport to someone? Work with a partner and try to explain a sport to each other.

Now listen to this woman talk about her favorite sport, jogging.

A Say whether the following statements are true or false.

1 The speaker prefers jogging to other sports.
2 She doesn't need a partner for jogging.
3 Jogging every day is recommended.
4 She listens to music as she jogs.

B Put "+" or "−" next to each item. "+" means you need the item to do the sport. "−" means you do not need it.

☐ a special place   ☐ proper clothing

☐ special equipment   ☐ a partner

☐ good shoes   ☐ a special time

C This time, put "+" to show something you should do and "−" to show something you shouldn't do.

☐ jog every day   ☐ eat just before or after you jog

☐ do warm-up exercises

☐ jog for a short time at first   ☐ have a cold drink just after you jog

PART 6   *You and Me*

Partner A: see page 64.   Partner B: see page 73.

PART 7   *Class Talk*

Now make a class report on your Partner A/Partner B interviews.

A: Tell the others about your partner's answers to b), d), and e). Give your answers to b) and d), too.

B: Tell the others about your partner's answers to 2), 3), and 5). Give your answers to 2) and 3) too.

Collect the information on the blackboard like this:

Like soccer?		Sports		Like tennis?		Sports we know a lot about	Keep in shape
Yes	No	Summer	Winter	Yes	No		

How many different sports do you know a lot about in your class?

unit 3 HOMES

A

B

C   D

A What sort of homes are these? Write A, B, C, and D.

1 .... a house   2 .... a camper

3 .... a houseboat 4 .... an apartment building

16

B Work with a partner and continue the list of advantages and disadvantages of living in each of these places.

	Advantages	Disadvantages
the house	It's big There's a yard	There's a lot of work to do in the yard
the camper		
the houseboat		
the apartment building		

C Would you like to live in these places? Maybe you'd like to live in one of them in the summer, but not in the winter. Or maybe you'd like to stay in one of them for a vacation. Use these words:

I'd like to live/stay in . . .
I'd prefer to live/stay in . . .   *because . . .*
I wouldn't like to live/stay in . . .

PART 2   *L i s t e n i n g*

What are the advantages and disadvantages of living alone? Talk with a partner and make a list. Then compare your list with others.

A Now listen to the cassette and say whether the following statements are true or false.

1 The woman has a large apartment in a new building.
2 She doesn't go out to eat all the time.
3 She likes to eat alone in restaurants.
4 She can cook what she likes.
5 She always feels lonely.

B Check the items the woman mentions.

☐ studio   ☐ balcony   ☐ dining room
☐ closet   ☐ bath   ☐ kitchen

C What kinds of food does she usually eat? Why?

17

A Greg is talking to Anna about her apartment. Put Anna's part of the conversation in the correct order. Greg starts:

1 Where do you live, Anna?	___ Yes, of course.
2 How big is it?	___ No, it's also a little cold—the heating system isn't very good.
3 And a kitchen and bathroom?	**1** In an apartment near the park.
4 Are the rooms big?	___ Mm, no . . . it's pretty cheap.
5 Is it expensive?	___ I'd like to have a small house near the ocean—with an orange tree in the yard.
6 And are you happy there?	___ Yes, I am—but it isn't perfect, you know.
7 Oh? What's wrong with it then?	___ The living room is, but the bedroom's pretty small. But it's OK.
8 Is that all?	___ It has two rooms.
9 Where would you really like to live?	___ Well, there's a lot of traffic on the street outside—so it's a little noisy.

B Read the dialog with a partner. Then go through it again, one person reading Greg's questions, and the other person giving *real* answers.

The "Homes for Everyone" society would like to make some new rules about houses and apartments. Decide for yourself if you think these rules are good or bad and then discuss your decisions and reasons with the rest of your class.

Good   Bad

— People with dogs and cats can't live in apartments. ☐ ☐

— Single people must live in one-room apartments. ☐ ☐

— Young people must live with their parents until they are 25, get married, or go away to college. ☐ ☐

— All college students can live free in dormitories paid for by the government. ☐ ☐

— Parents must move if their children leave home and their house or apartment is larger than necessary. ☐ ☐

L i s t e n i n g

How do you feel about your "home"? Is it a house, an apartment, a room? What is it like? How do you decorate it?

A Listen to a young man talk about his apartment. Answer the following questions with *yes* or *no*.

1 Does the man like his apartment?
2 Can he sit on his balcony?
3 Does he have a bed and a sofa?
4 Does he have a bathroom?
5 Is his studio comfortable?

B Circle the things he has in his studio.

bed   bookcases   computer   stereo   TV   stove   washing machine

C Complete the floor plan of the studio. Use the words in the box.

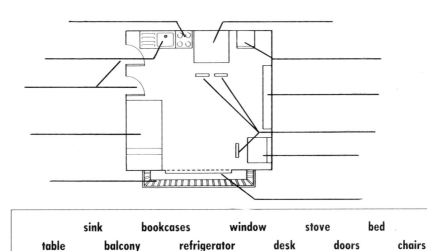

sink	bookcases	window	stove	bed
table	balcony	refrigerator	desk	doors	chairs

PART 6 *Y o u   a n d   M e*

Partner A: see page 65.   Partner B: see page 74.

PART 7 *C l a s s   T a l k*

What are typical houses like in your country?
— Talk about the rooms, the heating system, the outside of the building, etc.
— Compare houses in your country with houses in another country where they are different.
— How (and why) are they different?

unit 4 JOBS

Pictures to Talk About

A Look at these pictures of people working. Match the correct picture to the name of the job.

A

B

C

D

E

F

1 .... taxi driver **2** .... singer **3** ....vet

4 .... flight attendant **5** .... teacher **6** ....computer programmer

B Which of the jobs do you think these words go with?

regular working hours: ....D F.... inside: ....

uniform: .... noisy: ....

alone: .... dangerous: ....

away from home: .... stressful: ....

C Talk about all six jobs using the following words:

I expect he/she often . . . *I'm sure he/she always has to . . .*
He/she is lucky because . . . *I hope he/she never . . .*
It must be awful to have to . . . *I expect he/she is happy . . .*

20

C l a s s   T a l k

Which jobs in your country do you think are:

—very exciting?   —very well paid?
—very boring?   —very glamorous?
—very stressful?   —very dangerous?

PART 3 *L i s t e n i n g*

When you go to a job interview, you have to answer lots of questions.
Work with a partner and write five questions you think you might be
asked during an interview. For example:
What kind of work have you done before?

Now listen to the cassette. A college student is being interviewed
for a part-time job as a swimming instructor by the manager of the
swimming school.

A Say whether the following statements are true or false.

1 The student wants a part-time job as a manager of a swimming
   team.
2 The student teaches swimming.
3 She has no purpose for wanting the job.
4 Saturday is a popular day for swimming classes.
5 She has little work experience.
6 She doesn't get the job.

B Write in the appropriate column the things the student says about
herself.

Past	Now	Future

An Interview for a Job

A The woman you can see in this picture is interviewing the young man for a job. She's the manager of a hotel in a mountain resort. The job is a summer job at the reception desk of the hotel. Both the interviewer and the interviewee have several questions to ask. Work together with a partner to write down the questions.

Example: The interviewer would like to know how old the man is.

How old are you?

She would like to know if the young man can speak French or Spanish.

....

She needs to know if he can type. She wants to know if he can drive.

....

She'd like to know who his last employer was.

....

She wants to know what his last job was.

....

She wants to know if he can start next Monday.

....

The young man would like to know how many people the hotel employs.

....

He'd like to know if he will sometimes have to work at night.

....

He wants to know how many hours a week he'll have to work.

....

He wants to know how many days off he'll have.

....

He wants to know what his salary will be.

....

B Now take the parts of the interviewer and interviewee and ask and answer these questions.

L i s t e n i n g

What would be an ideal job for you? What would you like to have or do in your ideal job? For example:

—travel overseas
—good pay
—help others

Make a list and then discuss your list with others in your class.

Now listen to the cassette. In the conversation, you will hear a man and a woman talking.

A Answer these questions with *yes, no,* or *I don't know.*

1 The man and the woman know each other very well.
2 He works for an airline.
3 The woman likes her job.
4 The woman has traveled to many places.

B The woman says some positive things about her job. Check (✓) the ones mentioned.

☐ flying overseas

☐ going to different places

☐ long flights

☐ beautiful sights

☐ sick passengers

☐ annoying passengers

☐ discounts on hotels and flights

C Listen again and circle the item in the list that is the most *negative* aspect of her job.

PART 6 *Y o u   a n d   M e*

Partner A: see page 65.   Partner B: see page 74.

PART 7 *C l a s s   T a l k*

What is the work situation like in your country?

—Are a lot of people out of work?
—What help can a person get if he/she doesn't have a job?
—How do people try to find jobs?
—Do men and women do similar jobs?

unit 5 F O O D

PART 1 *Pictures to Talk About*

A Here are four photographs of people who are eating. None of the people are at home.

Where are the people in the pictures? Write A, B, C, and D here:

1 .... in a cafeteria   2 .... in a field or park

3 .... on the street   4 .... in a restaurant

B Talk about the differences between the places, the food, the cost, and the comfort of A, B, C, and D.

Vocabulary

These twelve words could be used to describe the food, the service, and the inside of a restaurant. Divide them into three groups of four words, using each word only once.

slow   attractive   friendly   interesting   modern   awful   elegant   over-cooked   unfriendly   shabby   excellent   fast

The food	The service	The inside of the restaurant

Which of these words say something positive about the restaurant, and which say something negative? Which do you think is the most positive and the most negative word in each group? Are there any words here that could be put in all three groups?

Listening

What kind of restaurant do you like to go to? What do you look for: food, service, atmosphere? Which is most important to you?

Now listen to two friends talking about eating in a restaurant.

A Circle the best summary statement.

1 The speakers are comparing their visits to a restaurant.
2 One of the speakers is unhappy about his visit to a restaurant.
3 One of the speakers is recommending a particular restaurant.

B Put "−" next to what is negative about the restaurant. Put "+" next to what is positive about the restaurant.

☐ service   ☐ dessert

☐ food   ☐ inside of the restaurant

C Match the adjectives with the nouns.

1 French   **a** places
2 terrible   **b** atmosphere
3 salty   **c** chocolate mousse
4 modern   **d** restaurant
5 old-fashioned   **e** food
6 wonderful   **f** service

PART 4   *Y o u   a n d   M e*

A Talk to your partner about food, and make a list for both of you. Ask about the following:

	Me	My partner
your favorite food		
something you don't like to eat		
a drink that you don't like		
a national specialty that you like		
your specialty (as a cook!)		

B What do you think is typical food or drink from these countries?

France ....   Japan ....

Italy ....   the U.S. ....

Korea ....   India ....

China ....   Mexico ....

England ....   Spain ....

Compare your list with that of a different partner.

PART 5   *C l a s s   T a l k*

Tell the others five facts about the last breakfast, lunch, or dinner you had.
—What did you eat?
—Where did you eat?
—Who were you with?
etc.

PART 6   *L i s t e n i n g*

Can you cook? How did you learn? (By watching someone? By studying with someone? By using a cookbook?) Which is the easiest/ most difficult way to learn to cook, in your opinion? Why?

Now listen to a recipe for making lasagna. Before you listen, match the following words to the pictures.

chop   sprinkle   grate   slice

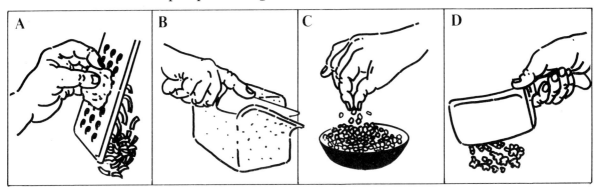

A Put the steps for making lasagna in order by numbering them 1–8.

☐ bake it in the oven

☐ cook the ground meat

☐ slice the mozzarella cheese

☐ let it stand for ten minutes

☐ cook the noodles

☐ get everything ready

☐ fill the baking dish

☐ chop the parsley

B Listen again and underline the mistakes in the following paragraph.

Now, in the top of the baking dish, put a thick layer of the tomato sauce. Then put down a layer of cheese. Sprinkle some of the ground meat over the cheese. Put some ricotta cheese on the meat and then slices of the ricotta cheese here and there over the meat as well. Finally, sprinkle some Parmesan cheese and a little chopped onion over all of it.

PART 7   *You and Me*

Partner A: see page 66.   Partner B: see page 75.

PART 8   *Class Talk*

Talk about the food and ways of cooking that are popular in your country and about your experiences with food from other countries.

unit 6 M O N E Y

PART 1 *M o n e y   i n   M o v i e s*

The comments about money that you can see below all come from movie dialogs. Work in groups of three or four to decide:

1 what the movie was about
2 who spoke these words
3 who listened to these words in the movie

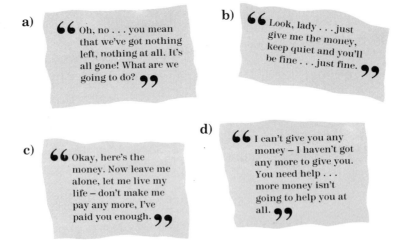

a) 66 Oh, no . . . you mean that we've got nothing left, nothing at all. It's all gone! What are we going to do? 99

b) 66 Look, lady . . . just give me the money, keep quiet and you'll be fine . . . just fine. 99

c) 66 Okay, here's the money. Now leave me alone, let me live my life – don't make me pay any more, I've paid you enough. 99

d) 66 I can't give you any money – I haven't got any more to give you. You need help . . . more money isn't going to help you at all. 99

Compare your ideas with others in your class.

PART 2 *L i s t e n i n g*

How do you use your pay or allowance? Do you save some of it? What are you saving for? Or do you spend all of it? What do you spend it on?

Now listen to this conversation between two students talking about saving and spending.

A Answer the questions.

1 One of the students is trying to persuade the other to save some of her money. Do you think he succeeds?
2 One of the students get money from her part-time job. Where else does she get money from?

B What do the students usually spend their money on? Circle the things mentioned.

CDs   cassettes   movies   food   cars   going out   travel

The Man with No Money!

A This man says he doesn't have any
money. There are several
reasons why he doesn't:

1 he doesn't work (he's too lazy)
2 he lives in an expensive apartment in
   the best part of town
3 he gambles
4 he smokes a lot of big cigars
5 he has three cars—one old
   Rolls Royce, one sports car, and
   one family car.

What do you think he should do?

Example:
I think he should look for a job.

Suggest three ways he could solve his other problems. Use the words
should and *shouldn't* as often as you can.

B Work with a partner to think of three more possible reasons why
this man doesn't have any money.

C Read your reasons to the class and listen to their ideas about what
he should do to help himself.

PART 4 *Class Talk*

Decide for yourself if you agree or disagree with these statements.

	Agree	Disagree
—Children should get money for doing jobs at home.	☐	☐
—All children should have an allowance to spend as they want.	☐	☐
—Children should learn how to save and how to budget.	☐	☐
—Children shouldn't play games where the aim is to win money.	☐	☐

Discuss your decisions with the other people in your class.
Tell the others about the experiences you had with money when you
were a child.

Vocabulary

A What forms of money are these? You need these letters to complete the words:

a d d e e h i i i l l n o c r r s t k

1 c.......................... 2 c.......................... 3 b.......................... 4 c............ c ....

1 Which two of these four are also called cash?
2 Which of these four do you have with you at the moment?
3 Which of these do you normally use?
4 Are any of these not used in your country?
5 Which of these are useful when you travel abroad?

B Which of these countries do you think have "dollars," "yen," or "pesos?" Match the country with its currency.

1 Australia	**a**	baht
2 Hong Kong	**b**	yuan
3 Japan	**c**	pounds sterling
4 China	**d**	dollars
5 Thailand	**e**	yen
6 Mexico	**f**	pesos
7 South Korea	**g**	won
8 England	**h**	dollars

PART 6 *Listening*

When you travel overseas, you need to plan carefully. Discuss with a partner some of the things you need to have for a trip and make a list.

Here are some suggestions:

passport   visa   money

Compare your list with two or three others.

Now listen to a woman exchanging money and buying travelers checks in a bank in the U.S.

A Which is the best summary of the conversation?

1 The woman is going to Australia on business and she needs travelers checks and cash. She will arrive in Australia late.

2 The woman wants to cash some Australian travelers checks. She has travelers checks already. She will exchange money at the airport.

B Answer the questions with *yes* or *no*.

1 Does the woman want to cash some travelers checks?
2 Does she want to get some Australian dollars?
3 Will she arrive in Australia too late to get some Australian money?
4 Does she want $1000 in cash?
5 Can she get travelers checks in $10s, $20s, or $100s?

PART 7 *Y o u   a n d   M e*

Partner A: see page 67.   Partner B: see page 76.

PART 8 *C l a s s   T a l k*

When we travel overseas, we have to spend money on a lot of things. We have to pay for travel to our destination (airplane/ship/train, etc.) and our hotel once we get there. Then, in some countries, we have to tip people for services, such as in restaurants or taxis.

With a partner, choose some place outside your own country you would like to visit. Then make a list of how you would use your money.

Necessary expenses	Optional expenses
food	*sun tan lotion*

Compare your list with others to see if you've forgotten anything.

unit 7 CLOTHES AND LOOKS

PART 1

Pictures to Talk About

When we see people we often think that we know something about them just by their appearance. Look at these pictures. What can you say about the people after looking at the photographs?

Useful language:
> *He/she looks . . .*
> *I'm sure he/she . . .*
> *I bct he/she . . .*

A

B

C

D

32

L i s t e n i n g

Some people have to wear uniforms for work or school. What do you think are the advantages and disadvantages of wearing a uniform?

Now listen to a nurse talking about wearing a uniform.

A Is the nurse unhappy about wearing a uniform for her work?

B Which of the following are mentioned as advantages of wearing a uniform?

practical   inexpensive   comfortable
easy to take care of   attractive   impressive

C What is the one disadvantage she mentions?

PART 3 *C l a s s   T a l k*

Make a list of people who wear uniforms.

People who wear uniforms for their jobs	People who wear uniforms for other reasons

Which uniforms do you think are attractive, and which are unattractive?

PART 4 *F a c e s*

A Work with a partner. Draw four faces on a piece of paper, like this but bigger:

(L)   with a nose in the middle.

Now choose a pair of eyes with eyebrows and a mouth to make your faces look a) sad b) happy c) surprised d) angry.

B Now you and your partner should think of four very short stories to explain why your four people are feeling the way they are.

C Tell these stories to two other people and listen to their explanations too. Choose which of their stories you like the best.

PART 5 *L i s t e n i n g*

What does it mean when we say someone is "good looking," "attractive," or "handsome?" Is it the person's clothes or physical characteristics? What are some advantages and disadvantages of being "good looking?"

Now listen to a conversation between two women.

A Choose the best summary of the conversation.

1 The two women talk about a handsome man in the yoga class, and a beautiful woman.
2 One of the women thinks being good-looking is a disadvantage because people bother you.
3 Both of the women are interested in studying yoga to meet attractive people.

B Say whether the following statements are true or false.

1 Both of the women are taking yoga lessons.
2 There's a handsome young man in the class.
3 Emi Kubota is an attractive woman.
4 One of the women went out for dinner with Emi.
5 A lot of men wanted to talk with Emi.

PART 6 *D e s c r i b i n g P e o p l e*

A What does he look like? What does she look like? Match the drawings below to the adjectives on the right.

hair:
- [ ] long and straight
- [ ] short and curly
- [ ] shoulder-length and wavy

face:
- [ ] round
- [ ] square
- [ ] oval

some other useful words:
- [ ] glasses
- [ ] beard
- [ ] moustache

B Work with a partner and write a description of his/her face and head. Now mix up all the papers in your class or group. Each person should take one. Make sure you don't have the description you wrote. Listen to the descriptions and write down the names of the people you think are being described.

PART 7 *V o c a b u l a r y*

❝ I went shopping for some clothes yesterday. I wanted to buy a sweater, a raincoat, a pair of shoes, and a skirt. But everything I tried on was wrong . . . too big or too small or there was something else wrong. In the end, I didn't buy anything. **❞**

Find the opposites of these adjectives in the box (the letters of the words are mixed up). Work with someone else if you want.

1 big.....*small*.........   5 ordinary ....
2 long.......................   6 casual ....
3 heavy ....   7 expensive ....
4 old-fashioned ....

htlgi	epahc
mnrdoe	pclaise
ohsrt	raomlf
~~sllam~~	

Use these adjectives to talk about the things she tried on.
Example: She tried on a sweater but it was too big. She really wanted a smaller one.

PART 8 *Y o u   a n d   M e*

Partner A: see page 67.   Partner B: see page 76.

PART 9 *C l a s s   T a l k*

Make a report on your Partner A/Partner B interviews.

A: Tell the others about your partner's answers to questions b) and c). Give your answers to these questions too.

B: Tell the others about your partner's answers to questions 1) and 4). Give your answers to these questions too.

Collect the information on the blackboard like this:

Comfortable clothes	Uncomfortable clothes	Newest item	Where he/she buys clothes

unit 8 FAMILIES

PART 1 *Opinions*

A These two college students come from very different families. Here's what they think about their family situations.

"I'm from the U.S. I'm an only child, so when I was young I was often with adults—my parents or their friends. Both of my parents worked. They gave me quite a lot of spending money, and when I was sixteen they bought me a car. I don't think I was ever lonely—there were lots of other kids in the neighborhood and we always played together on weekends and after school."

"I'm from Australia, but my family is from India. My family is very big— there are six children, our parents, and my grandmother all in one house. I have to share a bedroom with two sisters, and we really enjoy that. Big families are fun. You can't get lonely, that's for sure. We girls share our clothes, and we usually share one big birthday party too."

B Can you understand the way these two young people feel? Work in groups of four to find as many advantages and disadvantages as you can in the situation of the only child, and as many advantages and disadvantages as you can in the situation of the young woman from the large family.

Only child		Large family	
Advantages	**Disadvantages**	**Advantages**	**Disadvantages**

Now present your ideas to the others. Each person in the group can take one of the lists and present it like this:

Example (only child—advantages):
I'm an only child and I'm happy that I don't have any brothers or sisters. My parents pay a lot of attention to me and they give me . . . (etc.)

PART 2   *L i s t e n i n g*

Discuss some of your memories about your childhood in groups. How many people were living at home? Where did you go on vacations? Who did all of the chores?

Now listen to one woman talk about her childhood.

A Number the topics 1–3 in the order in which the woman talks about them.

☐ summer vacation

☐ fighting with her brother

☐ chores at home

B Say whether the following statements are true or false.

1 There were five people in the family.
2 All the family members helped out at home.
3 The children sometimes fought.
4 The girls did their brother's work for him.
5 The family went away every summer to Canada.
6 They enjoyed outdoor sports together.

C Answer the questions.

1 What two chores does the woman mention?
2 What four sports does she mention?

Family Memories

Work with a partner. Ask him/her the following questions and make a note of all his/her answers.

_____'s answers:

How many children, including you, are there in your family?	
Are you the oldest child, the youngest child, or somewhere in the middle?	
What is the age difference between the oldest child and the youngest?	
What do you think is an ideal number of children to have in a family?	
What is an advantage of your position in the family?	
What is a disadvantage of your position in the family?	

Look at the answers that you got from your partner and compare them with the answers he/she got from you. How many of your answers are the same? How similar are your families?

PART 4 *Vocabulary*

Copy and complete the chart by writing the words in the correct box.

brother	daughter-in-law	sister-in-law	wife	grandmother
cousin	grandfather	granddaughter	mother	daughter
uncle	father-in-law	son-in-law	niece	grandson
son	brother-in-law	mother-in-law	aunt	husband
sister	stepmother	stepfather	nephew	father

Female relatives	Male relatives

L i s t e n i n g

Try to make a list of all the members of your family: cousins, aunts, uncles, etc. Compare your list with your partner's. Talk about your family with others in your class.

Now listen to a grandmother talking with one of her grandchildren.

A Say whether the following statements are true or false.

1 The grandmother is not very old.
2 She has a lot of grandchildren and some great-grandchildren.
3 Her grandchildren all live near her.
4 She is still active.
5 She likes to travel.

B Her grandchildren live in various places. Circle the places mentioned.

France   Alaska   Texas   California   Japan

C Complete these sentences.

1 There are two main topics in the conversation:

.... and ....

2 One reason the grandmother can't remember the names of her

grandchildren and great-grandchildren is because ....

....

3 The grandmother is very active. She wants to ....

....

PART 6 *Y o u   a n d   M e*

Partner A: see page 68.   Partner B: see page 77.

PART 7 *C l a s s   T a l k*

What special days do you celebrate in your country?

—Are these days usually celebrated with relatives or with friends?
—How are they celebrated?
—How about more personal special days such as birthdays and wedding anniversaries? How do you celebrate those days?

unit 9 EDUCATION

A Here are six comments about going to school in the United States. Work in groups of four or five, and discuss each comment. You can see a grid under the comments. Fill in the number of people in your group who can make the same comments as these about themselves, and the number who say that things were different for them.

1. I went to a private school.

2. I started school when I was six. Before that I was in pre-school.

3. We went to school five days a week – there wasn't any school on Saturdays or Sundays.

4. I started learning my first foreign language when I was thirteen.

5. I had to wear a uniform when I was in school.

6. We always had lunch at school – a cooked meal in the cafeteria. The food was OK, I guess.

COMMENT:	1	2	3	4	5	6
It was like this for me when I was at school.						
It was different for me when I was at school.						

B If any of these things were different for you, what do you think the advantages and disadvantages of the system in the U.S. might be?

L i s t e n i n g

How do you learn something new? Some people enroll in a class; others read a book and study on their own. Discuss different ways to learn a new subject like Chinese or art history, or a new skill such as typing or cooking.

Now listen to a young woman talk about how she learns new things.

A The speaker talks about three different topics. Put them in order.

☐ learning a language

☐ learning a skill

☐ learning abstract subjects

B What examples of skills does the speaker give, and what examples of abstract subjects? Fill in the chart using the words from the box below.

Skills	Abstract subjects

psychology   using a word processor   economics
using a computer   repairing a bicycle

C Is the following information in the passage? Answer *yes* or *no*.

1 Some people use mostly their ears, others mostly their eyes, when studying languages.
2 The speaker depends mostly on her eyes.
3 Having someone show how to do something is useful.
4 Reading an instruction manual is always useless.
5 The speaker needs to talk about subjects like economics to learn them.
6 Writing is also useful for learning a new subject.
7 Learning by doing is helpful.

Vocabulary

Here are some of the courses that American high school students usually take at school. Can you work out what they are?

1 t h i s o y r   H _ _ _ _ _ Y
2 p a h s s i n   S _ _ _ _ _ H
3 p i s s h y c   P _ _ _ _ _ S
4 s m c i u   M _ _ _ C
5 h e s g n l i   E _ _ _ _ _ H
6 s a a t c m h m e i t   M _ _ _ _ _ _ _ _ S
7 y i n t p g   T _ _ _ _ G
8 y m t r h c e i s   C _ _ _ _ _ _ Y

You and Learning

How do you feel about learning now? Answer these questions for yourself and then ask at least two other people what their answers are.

---

1 Is English the only subject you're studying now?

☐ yes   ☐ no

What other subject(s) are you studying?...

....

2 How long have you been studying English?

☐ years

3 Can you speak any other foreign languages?

☐ yes   ☐ no

4 Why are you learning English? (you can choose more than one here, if you want)

☐ because I want to   ☐ for travel

☐ because I have to   ☐ because there's an English-speaker in my family or who is a friend

☐ for my work

☐ to take an examination   ☐ to understand books, movies, or songs better

☐ for my studies   ☐ other (what?)

5 Is there anything else you'd like to learn? (e.g. a language, a hobby, or a skill)

☐ no   ☐ yes

What would you like to learn?...

PART 5 *Class Talk*

Make a list together (on the blackboard) of all the ways in which you can learn something new at your age in your country. Think about:
— various types of schools
— learning from the radio, etc.

PART 6 *Listening*

Imagine that you have an opportunity to learn something new. What would you choose to learn? Ballet dancing? Playing the guitar?

Now listen to a telephone conversation between the receptionist at a dance school and a new student.

A Say whether the following statements are true or false.
1 The man calling wants to take dancing lessons.
2 The man has never studied dance before.
3 He wants to take lessons twice a week.
4 The best class for him is Thursday from 7 to 9 P.M.

B This is a summary of the telephone conversation. Listen to the cassette again and then complete the summary by filling in the blanks.

The man calling wants to take some .... dancing lessons. He wants to learn the fox trot, the ...., and the samba. .... evening is best for him, but the class that starts at .... is too early. The seven o'clock class is .... for him.

PART 7 *You and Me*

Partner A: see page 68.   Partner B: see page 77.

PART 8 *Class Talk*

Now make a class report on your Partner A/Partner B interviews.
A: Tell the others about your partner's answers to e) and f).
B: Tell the others about your partner's answers to 1) and 2).

Best memory	Worst memory	Favorite subject	Most hated subject

A: Now answer questions e) and f) yourself, and add this new information to the report.

B: Answer questions 1) and 2) yourself, and complete the class report.

Was English anybody's favorite or most hated subject?

unit 10 THEN AND NOW

Questionnaire

A This is the beginning of a questionnaire about what people used to do when they were children, between six and ten years old. Work with two or three other people to add six more questions.

Name					
1 Did you use to live in the town where you live now?					
2 Did you use to go to school on Saturdays?					
3 Did you use to have birthday parties?					
4 Did you use to visit your grandmother or grandfather?					
5					
6					
7					
8					
9					
10					

B Now ask these questions to five people—if possible they should be five people who didn't work on the questions with you. Fill in their answers with a check (✓) if it is something they used to do, or a cross (×) if it is something they didn't use to do.

C Choose the two most interesting questions on the questionnaire and write a short report about each one. Add some information about yourself to each report.

Example: **Report on question 1**

Two people used to live in the town where they live now, and the other three used to live in a different place. I used to live in the same town too, but I moved away for ten years, and then came back again.

D Now choose one of these reports and read it to the rest of your class.

PART 2 *L i s t e n i n g*

Has the world changed a lot since you were a child? Have methods of transportation changed? Can you think of anything that wasn't invented when you were a child?

Now listen to the tape. Two friends are talking about their feelings about inventions and the modern world.

A Which is the best summary of the conversation?

1 Life in the past without modern inventions was better because there wasn't any pollution.
2 Traveling by bicycle is better than traveling by car or by plane because there is less stress.
3 Many of the inventions today cause pollution and stress, but some can be useful.

B Circle the inventions that are mentioned.

bicycles   ships   washing machines   calculators
cars   word processors   stereos   planes
trucks   microwave ovens   computers   dish washers

C There is one invention that one of the speakers would not want to give up. What is it?

Vocabulary

What can you see here? Write the words next to the numbers below.

airplanepocketcalculatorcarphotocopiertelevisionpaperbackwatch
telephonerefrigeratorwashingmachineelectriclightbulbballpointpen

1 ....   5 ....   9 ....

2 *an airplane*   6 ....   10 ....

3 ....   7 ....   11 ....

4 ....   8 ....   12 ....

PART 4 *Class Talk*

How important are the things in Part 3 to you? Make a list (1 = most important, 12 = least important). Compare your list with several other people in your class. Which does your class think is the most important and least important?

How do you think your grandparents or your great-grandparents managed without these things? What did they have instead?

PART 5 *Listening*

When you were a child, was there a place that you liked very much? A friend's house? The pet shop in your neighborhood? A candy store?

Now listen to the tape. A woman is talking about one of her favorite places when she was a child.

A Check (✓) the reasons why her favorite place was the public library.

1 She had too many brothers and sisters at home. ☐

2 The library was quiet. ☐

3 She loved to read all kinds of books. ☐

4 The building was old and comfortable. ☐

5 She could walk to the library from home. ☐

6 Her parents didn't like her going to the library. ☐

B Now listen again and answer these questions briefly.

1 What kind of house did she live in?
2 How often did she go to the library?
3 Did people know her at the library?
4 What was the library building like?

PART 6 *You and Me*

Partner A: see page 69.   Partner B: see page 78.

PART 7 *Class Talk*

Think back to when you were a child. Tell the others about:

—a toy that you liked very much.
—a person who you liked very much.
—an activity that you liked to do very much.

unit 11 VACATIONS

PART 1 *Opinions*

These two people are very positive about their vacations.

My sister and I always go on a package tour. They're really the best vacation to take. It's so easy—you pay your money and everything is organized for you. You don't have to think about anything at all.

We go camping every summer. We get a lot of fresh air and can travel and stop where we want. There are five of us in the family, and so camping is much cheaper than other types of vacation.

Work with a partner to make a list of the possible disadvantages of camping vacations or package tours. Then compare your list with others in your class.

Camping vacations	Package tours

L i s t e n i n g

What kind of vacation do you like to take? Do you like to do something adventurous? Or do you like a peaceful, quiet vacation?

Now listen to the tape. The conversation is about vacations.

A Answer the questions briefly.

1 How many people are talking?
2 Are they friends?
3 How many people went to Bali?
4 Do all the people who went to Bali work together?

B What are the different things the women did on their vacation in Bali?

Use the words in parentheses to help you.

1 .... (*beach*)

2 .... (*around the island*)

3 .... (*dancing*)

4 .... (*food*)

C Bali has a special culture. What cultural details are mentioned in this conversation?

t...........................   d...........................

c ....   m...........................

PART 3 *V a c a t i o n s   t o   R e m e m b e r*

Work in groups of three or four. Tell the other people in your group about your last vacation or a vacation you remember because it was special. The others will ask you questions . . . but you could tell them about:

—the way you traveled
—where you stayed
—the things you liked most about the vacation

Give plenty of details.

V o c a b u l a r y

A Match these symbols from hotel descriptions with the words.

___ tennis courts   ___ children welcome   ___ sauna   ___ conference room
___ bar   ___ pets welcome   ___ laundry service   ___ parking lot
___ golf course   _1_ restaurant   ___ swimming pool   ___ fishing
___ facilities for disabled people   ___ riding

B You want to reserve a hotel room, and you want the room to be very nice. Write five sentences about the room or hotel using *should*.

Example:

*The hotel should be near the sea.
The room should have a balcony.*

1 ....

2 ....

3 ....

4 ....

5 ....

Compare your list with others. How many different ideas are there in your class?

PART 5 *C l a s s   T a l k*

What differences do you think there probably are in the types of vacations the following people enjoy?

—a single person aged twenty
—a married couple with two young children
—a retired couple

What are they looking for when they go on vacation?
Collect all your comments together for the three categories.

L i s t e n i n g

When you first go to a country that's very different from your own, many things may be different. Can you add to this list?

language   food   climate   housing

What is the most difficult thing, in your opinion?

Now listen to one person's description about how he felt when he first went to a country different from his own.

A Say whether the following statements are true or false.

1 The speaker says that the first time you go to a very different country, it's a shock.
2 It is sometimes difficult to order food in a restaurant.
3 The desk clerks at the hotels often don't speak your language.
4 It is easy to travel in foreign countries.
5 Because of his experiences, the speaker doesn't want to travel anymore.

B Listen again and take notes. What kind of difficulties does the speaker mention?

PART 7 *Y o u   a n d   M e*

Partner A: see page 70.   Partner B: see page 78.

PART 8 *C l a s s   T a l k*

Have you ever traveled in any of the following ways? Tell the others of the experiences you've had.

unit 12 H E A L T H

Pictures to Talk About

A Some people might say that the people in these pictures are doing things that are bad for their health. Number these 1 to 6, starting with what you think is the worst thing to do.

B Work with a partner to decide on one sentence for each picture beginning with *You shouldn't . . .*

Example:
You shouldn't take too many pills.

You shouldn't ....

You shouldn't ....

You shouldn't ....

You shouldn't ....

You shouldn't ....

Compare sentences with two other students.

C Perhaps it's just a question of doing these things too often or too much. Work with your partner to decide what limits you could put on each of the activities in the pictures.

Example:
Lying in the sun is okay, but not for the whole day.

PART 2 *L i s t e n i n g*

Stress is a very common problem in the modern world. Do you suffer from stress? If so, how do you get relief from it? Collect different ways to relieve stress by asking at least three others in your class. Make a list and then compare lists with a partner.

Now listen to this conversation.

A Answer the following questions briefly.

1 How many people are talking? Are they friends?
2 What is the topic of their conversation?

B Say briefly why one of the men has not been very well recently.

C Match the speakers with their ways of relieving stress.

1 first speaker	**a** tennis
2 second speaker	**b** jogging
	c swimming
	d working out in the gym

D One of the speakers is trying to give advice. Does he succeed? What do they agree to do at the end of the conversation?

PART 3 *C l a s s   T a l k*

Divide into groups. Each group should take one of the following topics:

relaxation   physical exercise   food and drink

—Discuss the things that you do that are good for you or bad for you. One person in each group should make notes so that he/she can report the comments of the group to the rest of the class.
—Do the people who do things that are bad for them want to change? Have they tried to change?

Tips for Health

Useful language:
Never [work]...
Try to [work]...
Avoid [working]...
Make a point of [working]...
Make sure you [work]...
Don't [work]...

Work in groups of three or four. Add nine more ideas to this list of golden rules for health. The list is for young people who are just starting their first jobs in offices.

GOLDEN RULES FOR YOUR HEALTH

1 **Try to walk for at least fifteen minutes on your way to and from work.**

2

3

4

5

6

7

8

9

10

Compare your list with another group's list.

PART 5 *Listening*

More and more, people can't smoke in certain places: on subway platforms, on flights inside the U.S. of less than two hours. What changes have you noticed recently? What do you think of this new trend?

Now listen to two young people talking about smoking.

A What is the first speaker trying to do in this conversation? Does he succeed? Answer briefly.

B Say whether the following statements are true or false.

1 The first speaker got caught smoking by his swimming coach.
2 He stopped smoking because he wanted to be a good swimmer.
3 Some people believe smoking is very masculine.
4 You can't become addicted to cigarettes.
5 His girlfriend wants him to stop smoking.

C Parts of the conversation have been jumbled. What is the correct order? Number them 1–5.

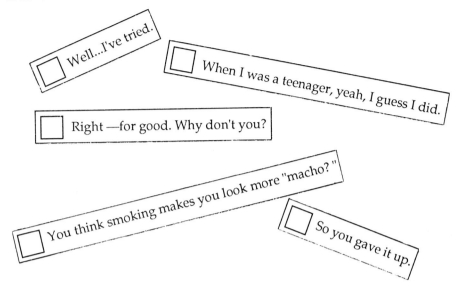

PART 6 *You and Me*

Partner A: see page 71. Partner B: see page 79.

PART 7 *Class Talk*

Which of these do you think are real health risks in your society?

smoking   drinking alcohol   polluted air   chemicals   noise
drugs and medicines   stress

Can you suggest ways of reducing these risks?
Can you think of any other risks?

unit 13 FREE TIME

PART 1 *Questionnaire*

A This is the beginning of a questionnaire about entertainment. Work with two or three other people to add six more questions beginning with *Have you ever . . .*

Some ideas: movies (different types of movies), circus, concert (different types of music), opera, theater (different types of plays), dancing.

	Name					
1 Have you ever been to a pop music concert?						
2 Have you ever seen people making a film?						
3 Have you ever been inside a radio or television studio?						
4 Have you ever acted in a play?						
5						
6						
7						
8						
9						
10						

B Now ask these questions to five people—if possible they should be five people who didn't work on the questions with you. Fill in their answers with a check (✓) or a cross (✗).

56

C Choose two of the positive answers you got, go back to the people who gave them, and ask two or three more questions.

For example, *Naomi* answered *yes* to question 4, so you know that she has acted in a play at some time in her past. Now you can ask some more questions about that.

Example:
What was the name of the play? Where did you act in this play? How old were you at the time? Were you nervous? Did you find it difficult to learn your lines? Who were you in the play? What sort of play was it?

D Use the information you get to write two short reports like this:

Example:
Naomi has acted in a play. She was fifteen years old at the time and the play was at her school. She didn't find it too difficult to learn the words because her family helped her. She was a little nervous on the first night.

E Now choose one of these reports and read it to the rest of your class.

PART 2 *L i s t e n i n g*

Discuss with two or three classmates the kind of entertainment you most enjoy and the kind you don't enjoy at all. Give your reasons.

Now listen to a TV reporter interviewing people on the street about their favorite forms of entertainment.

A Circle the forms of entertainment that are mentioned.

ballroom dancing   rock concerts   discos
classical music concerts   horror movies   foreign movies

B How many people does the reporter interview? ☐

From their voices, what kind of people are they? Put 1, 2, etc. next to the description to show Speaker 1, Speaker 2, etc.

☐ a young man, probably in his twenties

☐ an older man, well-educated

☐ a young career woman

☐ a teenage girl

☐ a middle-aged woman who studies music

C Why does the last person like a certain form of entertainment? Write down what she says.

C l a s s   T a l k

Tell the others about:
— a movie, play, concert, opera, musical, etc. that you have seen and that you remember very well
— a famous performer that you have seen

PART 4 *V o c a b u l a r y*

A What hobbies do these people have? Write in the vowels to complete the words.

The vowels you need:

a a a a a a a
a a a
e e e e e
e e
~~i~~ i i i i i i i
i i i i i
i i
o o o o o o o
u u u u

1 l.i.st....n....ng t.... m...s....c
2 ....rr....ng....ng fl....w....rs
3 t....k....ng ph....t....gr....phs
4 r........d....ng
5 v....s....t....ng m....s........ms

6 w....rk....ng ....n th.... g....rd....n
7 p....r....ch....t....ng
8 c....ll....ct....ng st....mps
9 cl....mb....ng
10 pl....y....ng th.... pi....n....

B Number these hobbies 1–10, starting with the one you think would interest you the most. Compare lists with a partner.

PART 5 *L i s t e n i n g*

What do you do with your free time? Do you exercise? Do you read for pleasure or to learn new things? Are you a member of a group to help other people? Make a list of different things to do with free time. Then try to give purposes for the different things.

Now listen to this conversation about free time activities.

A How many people are talking? What do you think their relationship is?

B Mark with a "+" the things mentioned that are a good use of one's free time, according to the women. Mark with a "−" those that aren't.

☐ telephones ☐ cooking

☐ televisions ☐ knitting

☐ sewing ☐ hiking

C Listen again, and then copy and complete these sentences.

1 One of the women likes to do ....: for example, ...
2 The other woman is involved in two groups: a .... group and an .... group.
3 The second group gives talks at .... and to ....

PART 6 *You and Me*

Partner A: see page 71.   Partner B: see page 79.

PART 7 *Class Talk*

What do you think are the differences in the ways these people spend their free time?

What is important to them at this point in their lives? What makes them choose to do some things and not to do others?

unit 14 FUTURE PLANS

Plans

A Read about these two people's plans for the future.

"I'm going to look for a new job and a new apartment next month. I'm going to look in the newspapers and ask all my friends for help. I'd like to move to another city or go and live in the country. Anyway, I'm not going to be here this time next year—I know that."

"I'm going to visit an old schoolfriend of mine next weekend. We're going to a tennis match on Saturday afternoon, but I don't know what we're going to do that night. On Sunday, we plan to stay at home until noon and then go to his parents' house for lunch. We're hoping to have a barbecue there."

Now look at the people below. Work with a partner to complete what they have to say about their plans. Use *going to, not going to, would like to, hope to,* and *plan to.*

"I'm going to retire next summer.
....
....
....
....
....
....
..........................."

"We're going to get married next year.
....
....
....
....
..........................."

B Now one of you take the part of the man who is going to retire, and the other take the part of either the man or woman on the right. Tell the rest of the class about your plans for the future.

L i s t e n i n g

Useful language:
I'm going to . . .
I'm not going to . . .
Next weekend I'd
like to . . .
Next year I plan
to . . .
Next week I'm
hoping to . . .

Work in groups of three or four. Tell the other people in your group about some plans you have for the future (if you don't have any, you could invent some really exciting ones!). Talk about later today, tomorrow, next weekend, next year, or even further into the future.

Now listen to three university students talking about their futures.

A Choose the best summary.

1 The three students talk first about places they want to travel to and then about where they would like to live for a while.
2 One of the students wants to travel in space, but the others don't. They would all like to travel to foreign countries, but none of them wants to live abroad.
3 The three students talk about places in the world where they would like to live and work. They don't like traveling in general.

B Match what the student wants to do with the name of the place.

1 medicine   **a** Japan
2 study and work   **b** The Philippines
3 agricultural technology **c** Africa

C Number (1–8) the names of the places in the order in which they are mentioned.

☐ The Mediterranean   ☐ China   ☐ Japan

☐ The Himalayas   ☐ India   ☐ Africa

☐ The Philippines   ☐ Nepal

C l a s s   T a l k

You're all going to live in a small, new country called Kazoonoland. This is the perfect moment for you to try and change the things you don't like in the society where you live now. In groups, discuss:

—how people are going to live and work in your society
—what your towns are going to be like
—what your schools and stores are going to be like
—what you're going to do with criminals

Compare your ideal country with that of other groups.

PART 4 *T h e   E n d   o f   t h e   C o u r s e*

Useful language:
Why don't we [go] . . . ?
How about [going] . . . ?
Shall we [go] . . . ?
I suggest that we [go] . . .
We could [go] . . .

Work in groups of about six to discuss the following problem. You'll need to make several suggestions so that the class will have a choice.

Your course is going to end in about five weeks' time. Make some plans for a class party. You don't want to spend *too* much money.

When you have plans for the party, exchange them with other groups in your class and make a definite class decision about what you're going to do together.

PART 5 *L i s t e n i n g*

What kinds of parties do you like to go to? Dance parties? Small dinner parties? What kinds of parties do you like to give? Pot luck parties with lots of friends? Or small ones with only a couple of friends?

Now listen to some friends who are planning a party.

A Agree or disagree with these statements. If you disagree, give a reason.

1 They are having a party to celebrate the end of the school year before the summer vacation.
2 Bob is reluctant to have the party at first.
3 They need to prepare a lot of food for the party.
4 Bob doesn't like Mike.
5 There are some overseas students who live across the street.
6 One of their friends sings Italian songs.
7 Bob wants everyone to meet his new girlfriend.

B Match the name of the person in Column A with the appropriate phrase in Column B.

A	B
1 Sheila	**a** plays the guitar
2 Mike	**b** Bob's new girlfriend
3 Yuki	**c** Tina's friend
4 José	**d** broke Bob's stereo
5 Kristina	**e** lives across the street

PART 6   *Y o u   a n d   M e*

Partner A: see page 72.   Partner B: see page 80.

PART 7   *C l a s s   T a l k*

Do you think it's a good idea to plan for the future? What things do you need to plan for:

—a trip you're going to take next weekend?
—your immediate future (the next few months)?
—your vacation in six months' time?
—the more distant future (five years from now, or when you retire)?

YOU AND ME: PARTNER A

Unit 1   Partner A

1 Role play. You are in a bookstore.
—you want a special book about Australia
—you only have $5 with you
—you have a credit card
—you could go home for more money and get back to the store just before five o'clock
—you accept the clerk's offer of help

2 Interview your partner. Make a note of his/her answers. Find out:
a) where he/she usually buys food
b) how often he/she goes to a supermarket
c) what he/she likes and dislikes about department stores
d) what he/she likes buying
e) what he/she hates buying

3 Answer your partner's questions. Give plenty of information.

Unit 2   Partner A

1 You and your partner have almost the same picture.
Talk to each other and find the eight differences.
Ask questions like:
Is there a/Are there any . . . in your picture?
Where is/are the . . .?
How many . . . are there?
What is . . . wearing/doing?

2 Interview your partner. Make a note of his/her answers. Find out:
a) which sports he/she watches on TV
b) if he/she likes soccer
c) if he/she ever reads the sports pages of the newspaper
d) if he/she prefers winter sports or summer sports
e) what he/she does to keep in shape

3 Answer your partner's questions. Give plenty of information.

1 Tell your partner where the furniture is in Room 2.
A = dining table and chairs   B = coffee table
C = armchair D = sofa E = television
F = stereo   G = bookcase

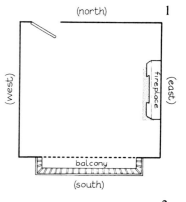

2 Your partner is going to tell you where the
furniture is in Room 1.   Draw the furniture in.
Useful language: *in the [northwest] corner,*
between, next to, opposite, on the [east] wall, behind

3 Which of these two rooms do you and your partner
think is the best?

4 Ask your partner these questions. Are his/her
answers positive or negative?

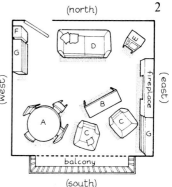

Do you live in a house with a yard?	+	−
Do you live with more than two other people?	+	−
Do you live near an airport?	+	−
Do you have a garage?	+	−
Is your house near a bus stop?	+	−
How many rooms does your house have?	+	−
Is your house in a big city?	+	−

How many negative answers did you get? ☐
Go back to the negative answers and ask another question.
Example: You don't live in a house with a yard—well, do you live in a house without
a yard or in an apartment?

5 Your partner is going to ask you seven questions now. Answer *yes* or *no.*

Unit 4   Partner A

---

1 Interview your partner. Find out if your partner has a job.

If the answer is yes, find out:

a) what his/her job is
b) if there is anything about the job
he/she doesn't enjoy
c) what hours he/she works
d) some details about his/her place of
work (office/school, etc.)
e) about the people he/she works
with

If the answer is no, find out:

a) why he/she doesn't have a job
b) what job he/she would like to have
c) if there is a job he/she wouldn't like to
have
d) if he/she expects to have a job in the
future
e) if he/she would like to work full time
or part time

2 Think of a job, but don't tell your partner what that job is. Your partner is going to ask you a maximum of fifteen questions to try to find out what job you're thinking of. You can only answer *yes* or *no*.
Example: If your partner asks *Do you work outdoors?* you can only answer *Yes, I do* or *No, I don't.*

3 You and your partner have almost the same picture. Talk to each other about the pictures and find the ten differences.
Ask questions like:

How many . . . are there?
Where is/are the . . .?
What is/are the . . . like?
Do you have a . . . in your picture?
Is/Are the . . . next to/on/under the . . .?

Unit 5   Partner A

1 Say these words to your partner one by one. Your partner will instantly say the first word he/she thinks of.
Example: You say *milk* and he/she may say *cow, cheese,* or *butter.* Write down the word your partner says:

soup	hamburger ....
Chinese food	breakfast ....
drink	vegetables ....
meat	picnic ....

2 Your partner has some words for you, too. Do the same thing and he/she will write down what you say.

3 Here is a list of the things you need to make your favorite pizza. Your partner wants to make the pizza this evening, but he/she has left the shopping list at home and can't remember all the things. You're on the phone now. Can you help your partner? Spell the words so he/she can write them down. It doesn't matter if you or your partner don't understand what all these things are. He/she can ask in the shop.

plain flour
yeast
salt
vegetable oil
tomatoes
green peppers
black olives
mozzarella cheese
anchovies
black or white pepper
marjoram

1 Interview your partner. Find out:

a) if he/she ever uses credit cards
b) what form of money he/she takes abroad
c) if he/she would like to work in a bank
d) where he/she got money from when he/she was in school.

2 Your partner has some questions for you.
Give plenty of information in your answers.

3 Role play. You're a cashier at a foreign exchange counter. You're speaking to a customer at the counter.

—greet the customer and offer to help
—write down the currencies and the amounts the customer wants
—find out if the customer has a credit card and offer an application form
—offer to have the money ready in an hour

1 Describe the woman on the right to your partner. If there are any words you don't know or can't remember, ask your partner for help.

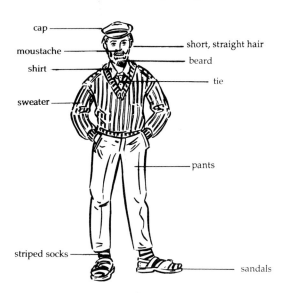

cap
moustache
shirt
sweater
short, straight hair
beard
tie
pants
striped socks
sandals

2 Your partner is going to describe the man on the left. You have the necessary words here, so if your partner can't remember a word, please help. Make sure that all the words you can see here are used.

3 Interview your partner. Make notes of his/her answers. Find out:
  a) if he/she really likes the clothes he/she is wearing today
  b) what sort of clothes he/she finds comfortable
  c) what sort of clothes he/she finds uncomfortable
  d) what his/her favorite color for clothes is
  e) how he/she feels about shopping for clothes

4 Answer your partner's questions. Give plenty of information.

Unit 8   Partner A

1 Here is part of Linda's family tree. Your partner has the other part. Ask questions to find out who the other twelve people are, and complete the tree. (The names in *italics* are all men's names.) Ask questions like: *Does Linda have any brothers or sisters? What are their names? How many . . .?*

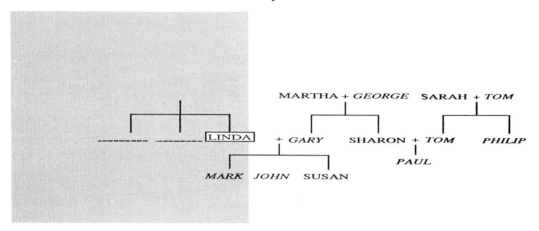

2 Now answer your partner's questions so that he/she can complete the tree too.

3 Work with your partner to decide how these people are related to Linda. Your partner has some names too.

Example: Susan   *She's Linda's daughter.*
  a) Patty   b) David   c) Charles   d) Mike   e) Emma

Unit 9   Partner A

1 Interview your partner. Make a note of his/her answers. Find out:

  a) at what age he/she started school   d) when he/she had to take examinations
  b) when he/she finished school   e) about his/her best memory of school
  c) what types of school he/she attended   f) about his/her worst memory of school

2 Answer your partner's questions. Give plenty of information.

3 Role play. You're the secretary at a language school. You're talking on the phone to someone who wants to take a language course.

— get the necessary information to complete this form
— you only have classes on Mondays to Fridays
— you have three classes at the correct level for the person on the phone:
Tuesday and Thursday 6–7:30 P.M.
Monday and Wednesday 7–9 P.M.
Wednesday and Friday 5:30–7 P.M.

Can you help the person on the phone?

LAST NAME: ....

FIRST NAME: ....

ADDRESS: ....

....

....

PHONE NUMBER: ....

LANGUAGE REQUIRED:

☐ English   ☐ Japanese

☐ Spanish   ☐ Chinese

☐ French   ☐ Korean

LEVEL: ☐ beginner

☐ intermediate

☐ advanced

REASON FOR LEARNING:

☐ business

☐ examination

☐ personal

Unit 10   Partner A

1 Write a few words in the boxes about your past, and then change books with your partner. Write down:

— a year that was important to you

— a place that was important to you

— a person who was important to you

— your best decision

— your worst mistake

2 Do you have your partner's book now?
Ask your partner to tell you more about the things in his/her book.

1 Make a list of five possible reasons why it's better for a family of four to travel long distances by car, and not by train.

a) ....

b) ....

c) ....

d) ....

e) ....

Your partner has a list of why it's better for a family to travel this distance by train. Compare your lists, and decide which *you* prefer.

2 Interview your partner. Ask the questions below, and if he/she answers *yes*, continue the conversation with at least two more questions:

Example:

Have you ever been to Europe? (Yes, I have.) When did you go there? Which country did you visit? Why . . .

Find out if he/she:
a) has ever been to Europe, Canada, or Australia
b) has ever been to a country with a very different culture than at home
c) has ever been to a country where the scenery is very different from at home
d) has ever been to a country without understanding the language at all
e) has ever gone abroad to learn a language or to work

3 Your partner has some questions to ask you. Give plenty of information in your answers.

Unit 12   Partner A

1 Before you and your partner start the interview below, answer the questions yourself with a check ($\checkmark$) or a cross ($\times$).

2 Interview your partner. Find out:

    Me My partner

  a) if he/she has ever broken a bone

  b) if he/she has ever had an accident

  c) if he/she has ever visited someone in the hospital

  d) if he/she has been sick this year

3 Now answer your partner's questions.

4 Now go back over both interviews with your partner. There is a total of eight questions. How many of these questions did you both answer with *yes* and how many did you both answer with *no*?

5 If your partner answered *yes* to any of your questions above, ask him/her to tell you more about what happened.

Unit 13   Partner A

1 Interview your partner. Try to discover as much as you can about his/her free time. Find out:
  a) what he/she usually does on Sundays
  b) if he/she does any sports regularly (or used to do any sports regularly)
  c) what sort of music he/she likes best, and what sort of reading material he/she usually chooses
  d) how he/she spends a typical weekday (in detail, and including the free time)
  e) what hobby or free time activity he/she would like to learn or take up (also find out why he/she hasn't done this up to now)

2 Your partner has some questions to ask you. Give plenty of information in your answers.

3 Are televisions, cars, and telephones good or bad for our free time? Make a list of at least two *positive* points for each thing. Now discuss these points with your partner (he/she has a list of negative points). What changes have these things brought with them?

4 Make a group of four with your partner and another A/B pair. Compare your lists of positive and negative points.

1 Before you start talking to your partner, choose the words you need to complete this story. Where you see "........" you can write in something yourself.

I'm going to take a vacation ☐ ....: ☐ later this year: I'm going to spend ☐ ....
☐ next year: ☐ 2 weeks
☐ a month

☐ .... ☐ ....
☐ in Hong Kong. I'm going to travel ☐ by plane.
☐ in Australia. ☐ by car.

I'm going on vacation ☐ ...., ☐ ....
☐ alone, and I'm/we're going to stay ☐ in a hotel.
☐ with a friend, ☐ with friends.

I'm/We're going to ☐ ....
☐ stay in one place all the time.
☐ travel around.

I usually send ☐ ....
☐ about 5 postcards when I'm on vacation,
☐ between 5 and 15

and I know I'm going to send one to ☐ ....
☐ my mother this time.
☐ my neighbor

2 Now ask your partner questions to find out the words that he/she has chosen.

Example: When are you going to take a vacation?

3 Your partner is going to ask you the questions now. Only answer questions that you think are correct. If your partner asks an incorrect question, help him/her to correct it before you answer it.

4 In groups of four, retell your partner's vacation plans to the others.

YOU AND ME: PARTNER B

Unit 1 Partner B

1 Role play. You work in a bookstore.
- — you have the book the customer wants
- — the price of the book is $12
- — you don't accept credit cards in your store
- — your store closes at four o'clock today
- — you can reserve the book for seven days
  if the customer pays 25 percent of the price
- — you have to fill in a form to reserve a book

2 Answer your partner's questions. Give plenty of information.

3 Interview your partner. Make a note of his/her answers. Find out:
1) whether he/she likes shopping in large supermarkets and shopping centers
2) what sort of store he/she would enjoy working in
3) what sort of store he/she would hate working in (and why)
4) which sort of stores he/she likes looking around in
5) how often he/she goes shopping

Unit 2 Partner B

1 You and your partner have almost the same picture.

Talk to each other and find the eight differences.

Ask questions like:
Is there/Are there any . . . in your picture?
Where is/are the . . . ?
How many . . . are there?
What is . . . wearing/doing?

2 Answer your partner's questions. Give plenty of information.

3 Interview your partner. Make a note of his/her answers. Find out:

1) if he/she is interested in sports (actively or passively)
2) if he/she likes tennis
3) which sport he/she knows a lot about
4) which sport he/she knows little about
5) what he/she does to keep in shape

73

1 Your partner is going to tell you where the furniture is in Room 2.
Draw the furniture in.
A = dining table and chairs B = coffee table
C = armchair D = sofa E = television F = stereo
G = bookcase

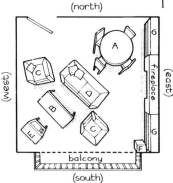

2 Tell your partner where the furniture is in Room 1.
Useful language: *in the [northeast corner], between,
next to, opposite, on the [east] wall, behind*

3 Which of these two rooms do you and your partner think
is the best?

4 Your partner is going to ask you seven questions.
Answer *yes* or *no*.

5 Ask your partner these questions. Are his/her answers
positive or negative?

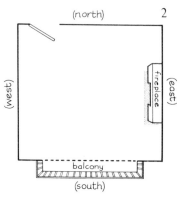

Do you live in a small town?	+	−
Do you live alone?	+	−
Does your house have three bedrooms?	+	−
Does your house have more than one floor?	+	−
Does your house have any disadvantages?	+	−
Do you like all the furniture you have?	+	−
Do you have a balcony?	+	−

How many negative answers did you get? ☐

Go back to the negative answers and ask another question.

Example: You don't live in a small town—well, how big is the place where you live?

1 Your partner has got some questions to ask you. Give plenty of information in
your answers.

2 Interview your partner. Your partner is thinking of a job. You can ask a
maximum of fifteen questions. Try to find out what the job is. Your partner can
only answer *yes* or *no*. Start with these questions. Find out:

a) if he/she works inside or outdoors (you can ask *Do you work outdoors?* and
your partner will answer *Yes, I do* or *No, I don't*)

b) if he/she works alone or with others (you can ask *Do you work alone?*)

c) if he/she handles money as part of the job

d) if he/she uses the phone a lot
e) if he/she stands or sits most of the time
    Now go on—you've got ten more questions, and then you can ask: *Are you a . . . ?*

3 You and your partner have almost the same picture. Talk to each other about the pictures and find the ten differences.
Ask questions like:

How many . . . are there?
Where is/are the . . . ?
What is/are the . . . like?
Do you have . . . in your picture?
Is/Are the . . . next to/on/under the . . . ?

Unit 5   Partner B

1 Your partner is going to say eight words or phrases to you one by one. Say the first word you think of in reply.

Example: Your partner says *milk* and you could say *cow, cheese,* or *butter,* etc.

2 Now you can do the same. Write down the word your partner says:

snack ....   traditional food ....
seafood ....   fish ....
Indian food ....   diet food ....
dessert ....   health food ....

3 You are at a supermarket. You want to make pizza this evening but you don't have a shopping list. You're on the phone to your partner who is at home. He/she has a list of things you need to make pizza. Find out which things you need to buy. Your partner can spell the difficult words for you.

At home you have:	In your shopping bag you have:	You need to buy:
salt	mozzarella cheese	....
white pepper	anchovies	....
plain flour	tomatoes	....
vegetable oil		....

1 Your partner has some questions to ask you. Give plenty of information in your answers.

2 Interview your partner. Find out:
  a) how much money he/she is carrying today
  b) whether he/she has changed money from one currency to another
  c) whether he/she usually pays by cash or by credit card in department stores
  d) how he/she saves money
  e) how often he/she goes to the bank

3 Role play. You're a customer at a foreign exchange counter. You're speaking to the cashier at the counter.
  — you want some travelers checks in U.S. dollars
  — you want some Taiwanese currency in cash
  — you're going to Taiwan for five days
  — you don't have a credit card and you don't want one
  — you're leaving tonight

1 Your partner is going to describe the woman on the right. You have the necessary words here, so if your partner can't remember a word, please help. Make sure that all the words you can see here are used.

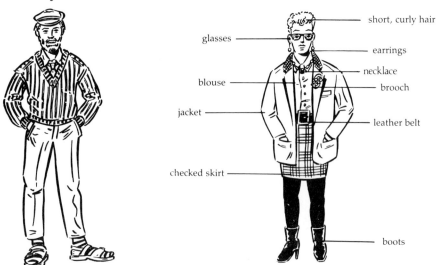

glasses

short, curly hair

earrings

necklace

blouse

brooch

jacket

leather belt

checked skirt

boots

2 Now describe the man on the left to your partner. If there are any words you don't know or can't remember, ask your partner for help.

3 Answer your partner's questions. Give plenty of information.

4 Interview your partner. Make a note of his/her answers. Find out:
1) what his/her newest item of clothing is
2) if he/she likes wearing jewelry
3) if he/she likes wearing perfume/cologne
4) where he/she usually buys clothes
5) what his/her biggest problem is when buying clothes

U n i t 8   P a r t n e r B

1 Here is part of Linda's family tree. Your partner has the other part, and is going to ask you questions about the information you have. (The names in *italics* are all men's names.)

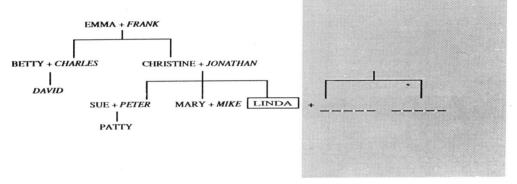

2 Now ask your partner questions about Linda's family so that you can find out who the other twelve people in the family are.
Ask questions like *Does Linda have a husband? What's his name? How many . . . ?*

3 Work with your partner to decide how these people are related to Linda. Your partner has some names too.

Example: Mary *She's Linda's sister.*
a) Sharon b) Paul c) Martha and George d) John e) Betty

U n i t 9   P a r t n e r B

1 Answer your partner's questions. Give plenty of information.

2 Interview your partner. Make a note of his/her answers. Find out:
1) what his/her favorite subject at school was
2) which subject he/she hated most
3) some information about the school he/she attended as a teenager
4) what his/her earliest memory of school is
5) if he/she still has contact with schoolfriends from the past

3 Role play. You want some information about a language course. You're telephoning a language school that has daytime and evening courses. You work full time and already have some regular evening arrangements.

MONDAY:
TUESDAY: *tennis 6-7*
WEDNESDAY:
THURSDAY: *discussion 7-10*
FRIDAY: *work?*

— you want to learn Spanish before your next vacation
— you're a complete beginner
— you'd like to go to school on Saturday mornings for three hours
— you definitely can't change your club meeting on Thursdays
— if really necessary, you could change your tennis lesson to 8 P.M.
— on Fridays you sometimes have to work late

Are you going to learn Spanish at this school?

Unit 10   Partner B

---

1 Write a few words in the boxes about your past, and then change books with your partner. Write down:

— a year that was important to you

— a place that was important to you

— a person who was important to you

— your best decision

— your worst mistake

2 Ask your partner to tell you more about the things in his/her book.

Unit 11   Partner B

---

1 Make a list of five possible reasons why it's better for a family of four to travel long distances by train, and not by car.

1) ....

2) ....

3) ....

4) ....

5) ....

Your partner has a list of five reasons why it is better for a family to travel this distance by car. Compare your lists and decide which *you* prefer.

2 Answer your partner's questions. Give plenty of information.

3 Interview your partner. Ask the questions below, and if he/she answers *yes*, continue the conversation with at least two more questions:

Example: Have you ever been camping? (Yes, I have.) Where did you camp? What was the weather like? What was the most difficult thing about camping? Did you . . .?

Find out if he/she:

    1) has ever been camping
    2) has ever gone on vacation alone
    3) has ever gone on a package tour
    4) has ever gone on vacation with a group of friends
    5) has ever had a vacation that wasn't enjoyable

Unit 12 Partner B

1 Before your partner interviews you, answer the questions yourself in the interview below with a check (✓) or a cross (✕).

2 Answer the questions that your partner has for you.

3 Interview your partner. Find out:

	Me	My partner
1) if he/she has been to see a doctor this year	☐	☐
2) if he/she has been to see a dentist this year	☐	☐
3) if he/she has had an accident this year	☐	☐
4) if he/she has been inside a hospital this year (as a patient, a visitor, or to work)	☐	☐

4 Now go back over both interviews with your partner. There is a total of eight questions. How many of these questions did you both answer with *yes* and how many did you both answer with *no*?

5 If your partner answered *yes* to any of your questions above, ask him/her to tell you more about what happened.

Unit 13 Partner B

1 Answer your partner's questions. Give plenty of information.

2 Tell your partner to look at the list of hobbies in Part 4 of this unit. Interview your partner. Ask:

    1) which of these hobbies he/she has already tried
    2) which of these hobbies he/she would definitely not like to try, and why
    3) which of these hobbies he/she would like to try
    4) if he/she finds any of them too dangerous, too expensive, or too difficult to learn
    5) what his/her favorite free time activity is

3 Are televisions, cars, and telephones good or bad for our free time? Make a list of at least two *negative* points for each thing. Now discuss these points with your partner (he/she has a list of positive points). What changes have these things brought with them?

4 Make a group of four with your partner and another A/B pair. Compare your lists of positive and negative points.

U n i t   1 4   P a r t n e r   B

1 Before you start talking to your partner, choose the words you need to complete this story. Where you see "........" you can write in something yourself.

☐ ....:
I'm going to take a vacation ☐ later this year: I'm going to spend ☐ ....
☐ next year: ☐ 2 weeks
                                                  ☐ a month

☐ ....
☐ in Hong Kong. I'm going to travel ☐ ....
☐ in Australia.   ☐ by plane.
                                        ☐ by car.

☐ ....,
I'm going on vacation ☐ alone,   and I'm/we're going to stay ☐ ....
☐ with a friend,   ☐ in a hotel.
                                             ☐ with friends.

☐ ....
I'm/We're going to ☐ stay in one place all the time.
☐ travel around.

☐ ....
I usually send ☐ about 5   postcards when I'm on vacation,
☐ between 5 and 15

☐ ....
and I know I'm going to send one to ☐ my mother   this time.
☐ my neighbor

2 Your partner is going to ask you some questions now to find out which words you have in your story. Only answer questions you think are correct. If your partner asks you an incorrect question, help him/her to correct it before you answer it.

3 Now ask your partner the questions to find out which words he/she has chosen. *Example: When are you going to take a vacation?*

4 In groups of four retell your partner's vacation plans to the others.

Transcripts

Unit 1, Part 2.

INTERVIEWER: Annette, you're a sophomore, aren't you?

ANNETTE: That's right. I'm a chemistry major.

INTERVIEWER: What kind of part-time job do you have?

ANNETTE: Well, I work in a bakery.

INTERVIEWER: Oh, really? Do you make bread?

ANNETTE: Oh, no. My job is to carry the bread and rolls and cakes through into the store and put them on the shelves so people can see them and choose what they want.

INTERVIEWER: Is that difficult?

ANNETTE: Well, it's not difficult. But sometimes, when the store is full of customers, people push, and I have to be careful not to drop anything on the floor.

INTERVIEWER: What else do you do?

ANNETTE: I'm also the cashier sometimes. We take turns at the different jobs.

INTERVIEWER: How many days do you work in the bakery?

ANNETTE: I'm there all day Saturday and then Monday and Thursday from 3 to 7. I work sixteen hours a week.

INTERVIEWER: Do you earn a lot of money in the bakery?

ANNETTE: Well, not very much . . . but I really enjoy working there.

INTERVIEWER: Oh?

ANNETTE: Yeah, I love to smell all the fresh-baked bread and cakes.

Unit 1, Part 4.

DONNA: Oh, Kim, I just don't know what to wear to Bob's party!

KIM: Well, Donna, how about buying something new?

DONNA: Something new? Well, yes, maybe I should. But I really don't know where to look.

KIM: Why don't you try the new shopping center? It has lots of small boutiques.

DONNA: Won't they be expensive?

KIM: Not really . . . and they may be having special opening sales.

DONNA: Well, maybe I should. I certainly don't like department stores.

KIM: I don't either. The clothes aren't very exciting.

DONNA: I guess I just don't like to go shopping.

KIM: I know what you mean . . . the stores are so crowded, and . . .

DONNA: And I can never find what I want.

KIM: But you want to look good for the party, right?

DONNA: Yes!

KIM: Hey, look: I'm free Thursday night, after work. Let's go shopping together.

DONNA: Thanks, Kim. I'd really appreciate that.

KIM: OK! We're going to find you something really special for the party!

Unit 2, Part 2.

Well, even when I was a little kid, I used to do dangerous things all the time, like climbing trees, and riding my bicycle really fast. And now I like dangerous sports. I love to ski as fast as I can down a steep mountain and this year I even tried ski jumping. When I first started college I thought I'd take it easy for a while, so I joined the badminton club—but I guess I got bored with that. Maybe it wasn't dangerous enough! Now I'm on the football team. It can be a pretty tough sport. The next thing I want to try is hang-gliding. I saw some people doing hang-gliding in an area just south of San Francisco, from the hills along the Pacific Ocean. It was great. It looked so peaceful, so beautiful. Of course, it can be really dangerous, but so far I haven't gotten hurt. So I want to try it. Then, after that, there's always Mount Everest. . .

Unit 2, Part 5.

I like jogging. It's cheap: you can do it almost anywhere. You don't have to have a special place or any special equipment. Of course, you have to have good running shoes and proper clothing, especially if you go jogging in the winter. But there aren't any rackets or balls or other special things to worry about. Also you can do it alone and at any time. Sometimes it's difficult to find a partner for tennis or a group to play volleyball.

You shouldn't go jogging every day. Three times a week or every other day is good. You need to do warm-up exercises and to start off slowly, only five to ten minutes at first. Then, if you only jog to keep in shape, a half hour is usually enough. Don't eat anything before or immediately after you go jogging. And don't drink anything really cold when you finish. It's a simple sport. A lot of people say it's boring. Sure, it can be . . . but that's why people jog with a Walkman. I have a great tape, a 45-minute "high energy" music tape. So I can listen to music *and* keep in shape.

Unit 3, Part 2.

INTERVIEWER:	So this is the first time you've lived alone.
NICOLE:	Yes. Up until now I've always lived with my family.
INTERVIEWER:	What kind of apartment do you have?
NICOLE:	I have a studio, a one-room apartment in an old apartment building. It's on the third floor. It's really nice . . . sunny, quiet. I like it a lot.
INTERVIEWER:	Do you have your own kitchen and bath?
NICOLE:	Yes, of course. And there's a balcony, though it's pretty small.
INTERVIEWER:	Do you do all your own cooking?
NICOLE:	Yes. Unless I go out with friends, I cook my own food, though I'm not a good cook . . . yet.
INTERVIEWER:	Do you sometimes go out by yourself to eat?
NICOLE:	Well, I don't like to eat out alone . . . and also here I can cook what I like.
INTERVIEWER:	What do you like to eat?
NICOLE:	Well, since I take dance lessons, I have to watch my weight. So I eat a lot of fish, salads, and fruit.
INTERVIEWER:	Don't you ever get lonely?
NICOLE:	Sometimes, but I wanted to learn to be independent. And I'm really learning to appreciate my family and friends more now.

Unit 3, Part 5.

Well, I have a really nice room, a studio apartment in fact. There's a big window on the south side, which opens out onto a balcony. I can sit out there in the summer time. My bed is against one wall. I cover it with a cloth I bought in Bali and some pillows so it looks like a sofa during the day. On the wall opposite the bed there's a desk right near the window with a chair, and then bookcases where I also put my stereo and a small TV. Along the back wall, the wall opposite the window, is the kitchen area, with a stove, refrigerator, and sink. In the center of that area I have a small table and two chairs. Right next to the bed there are two doors, one leading outside, the other to the bathroom. So it's a small studio, but it's very comfortable, and from the balcony I can see the park. It's nice to see green trees in the middle of the city.

Unit 4, Part 3.

MANAGER: Good afternoon. I understand you want to apply for a part-time job here as a swimming instructor.

STUDENT: Yes, I do. I've been a swimmer since I was six years old. And I was on the swimming team of my high school.

MANAGER: Have you actually taught swimming?

STUDENT: Yes, I have. For the last two years, I've been a volunteer instructor for handicapped children. The school for the handicapped is very near the university.

MANAGER: I see. And now you would like a job.

STUDENT: Yes. I want to save money so I can go to Spain next year to study Spanish.

MANAGER: Can you work on Saturdays? That's when we have several swimming classes for children.

STUDENT: Yes. I can also work two afternoons a week.

MANAGER: Have you ever worked before?

STUDENT: Oh, yes. I've done a variety of part-time jobs: baby-sitting, delivering newspapers, clerical work in an office, tutoring . . .

MANAGER: Well, that sounds good. Can you start next Saturday?

Unit 4, Part 5.

MAN: What kind of work do you do?

SUWALEE: I'm a flight attendant.

MAN: Oh really? That must be exciting. Do you fly overseas?

SUWALEE: Yes, I usually work on the Tokyo to San Francisco flight. And sometimes I go on to Singapore, Hong Kong, Beijing, or Seoul.

MAN: You're lucky. Boy, it must be great to fly all over the world to so many interesting places.

SUWALEE: Yeah—and flying into a city at sunset or sunrise . . . or New York at night when all the buildings are lit up . . . it's really beautiful. I love flying.

MAN: And you can stay for free in all the places you travel to?

SUWALEE: When I'm working, yes. But even when I'm not I can get discounts on hotels and flights for me and my family.

MAN: Oh, it must be a great job.
SUWALEE: Yes, most of the time it is, though it can be very tiring on long flights.
MAN: Do you ever have any trouble with the passengers?
SUWALEE: Well, sometimes they get sick, of course . . . but I guess the most annoying thing is when one passenger wants food, or something to drink, or a newspaper, or something else every five minutes. Sometimes I just want to yell at them to sit down and stop bothering me, but of course I can't—I have to keep that smile on my face even if I feel angry inside. That's hard.

Unit 5, Part 3.

RON: Have you been to Maude's, the new French restaurant?
CAROL: No, but I want to go. Have you?
RON: Yes, the other night. Don't waste your money.
CAROL: Really? Was it that bad?
RON: It was awful. You know how much I like French food.
CAROL: Me too. It's my favorite.
RON: Well, the service was just terrible. Too slow.
CAROL: And the food?
RON: Too salty. And the chicken we ordered wasn't cooked enough.
CAROL: That's terrible.
RON: Then the atmosphere was all wrong. The inside of the restaurant was too bright and modern, and the chairs weren't very comfortable.
CAROL: I don't like places like that. I like old-fashioned places.
RON: The only good thing was the dessert. The chocolate mousse was wonderful!

Unit 5, Part 6.

Before you start, you need to get everything ready. To make lasagna, you need lasagna noodles, tomato sauce, ground meat, grated Parmesan cheese, mozzarella cheese, ricotta cheese, and parsley. And of course you need a baking dish.

First cook the noodles in boiling water. Then cook the ground meat in a little olive oil. Chop the parsley and slice the mozzarella cheese into thin slices.

Now, in the bottom of the baking dish, put a thin layer of the tomato sauce. Then put down a layer of lasagna noodles. Sprinkle some of the ground meat over the noodles. Put some ricotta cheese on the meat and then slices of the mozzarella cheese here and there over the meat as well. Finally, sprinkle some Parmesan cheese and a little chopped parsley all over it.

Continue in the same way, layer on top of layer, until you fill the baking dish. Bake it at 350 degrees Fahrenheit for about 40 minutes. Let it stand for ten minutes. You can then cut it to serve.

Unit 6, Part 2.

KEVIN: Do you think you should spend all your money?
LORI: Why not? I earned it myself and so I should be able to spend it as I wish.

KEVIN: Don't your parents give you money for things?

LORI: Sometimes, yeah. But what about it? Don't you spend all of your money?

KEVIN: Well . . . I always feel I should save some of it.

LORI: Why?

KEVIN: I may need it for something really nice that I want to buy suddenly. Or to travel.

LORI: Well, if I decide I want to go somewhere, then I work hard and save all my money.

KEVIN: I see, but . . .

LORI: If I don't have any goal, then I go out a lot. I buy cassettes or CDs.

KEVIN: I do that too . . . I go to a lot of movies. But I guess I always save some of it. You should, too.

LORI: Give me a break, Kevin! You sound just like my Mom.

KEVIN: Don't you want to buy a car or travel?

LORI: Well, I do want to go to Mexico next summer . . .

KEVIN: Hey, your parents won't pay for something like that!

LORI: Yeah, well, maybe you're right.

Unit 6, Part 6.

CUSTOMER: I'd like to exchange some currency and buy some travelers checks, please.

TELLER: What currency do you have?

CUSTOMER: I have one hundred pounds from my last trip to England. I'd like some Australian dollars.

TELLER: Australian currency?

CUSTOMER: I'm going to Australia on business and my flight arrives too late to exchange money there.

TELLER: Oh, OK . . . and the travelers checks?

CUSTOMER: I'd like one thousand Australian dollars in travelers checks.

TELLER: Are you paying for that in cash?

CUSTOMER: I can give you a personal check, if that's all right—I have an account at this bank.

TELLER: That would be fine. OK then . . . how do you want the travelers checks? $10s, $20s, or $100s?

CUSTOMER: $100s, please.

TELLER: And when would you like to pick up the money?

CUSTOMER: Well, I'm leaving on Thursday, so I guess I'll have to pick it up Wednesday lunchtime. Can you have it ready by then?

TELLER: Yes, that's fine. Now if you'd just like to sign . . .

Unit 7, Part 2.

Sometimes people ask me if I really like wearing my white nurse's uniform all the time for work. I really can't say that it bothers me. I guess when I was in high school, one reason I decided I wanted to become a nurse was because I liked the white uniform. It looked impressive and important.

Nowadays there are all kinds of different styles for nurses' uniforms. And you can wear slacks and a shirt or top. You can even wear light blue uniforms, but I always stick with white. And uniforms are useful. In the big hospital where I work, people know immediately who I am from my uniform.

85

Uniforms are also practical. They're easy to take care of and comfortable to wear. And much cheaper than having to wear suits and dresses to work. I can spend my money on nice clothes for when I'm off duty.

The only disadvantage that I can see is the monotony, you know, wearing the same color, the same uniform day after day. But, as I say, I really don't mind at all.

Unit 7, Part 5.

SHARI:	I told you I've started taking yoga lessons, right?
JOANNE:	Yeah—how's it going?
SHARI:	Well, there's this incredibly handsome guy in the class.
JOANNE:	Oh, maybe I should start studying yoga too . . .
SHARI:	No, don't be silly. He's too young. And besides all the other women are after him.
JOANNE:	It's like my friend Emi—do you know her?
SHARI:	Ken's girlfriend?
JOANNE:	Yes.
SHARI:	Yeah—she's really attractive, isn't she?
JOANNE:	Right . . . well, we went out for dinner the other night because Ken's away on business, and I couldn't believe it!
SHARI:	Why, what happened?
JOANNE:	Well, as we were walking back from the restaurant to the subway station, several men stopped her, made comments to her. I guess she's used to it, but I was really surprised.
SHARI:	Yeah—maybe it's better to be normal-looking. Safer anyway.
JOANNE:	Maybe . . .

Unit 8, Part 2.

In my family, there was my mother and father, three children, a dog, and two cats. My father owned his own business and my mother was a school teacher. We children, my brother, my sister, and I, had to help out a lot at home. We had chores that we had to do every day, every week. But we would change every week. So one week I had to wash the dishes after supper, and then the next week I had to take care of the pets. My father also used to help, especially on weekends.

We used to have fights sometimes. My brother would sometimes try to make my sister and me do his chores. But we never did. He knew the two of us together were stronger than he was. We all helped each other with our homework, though. I was always good at math, but my sister was hopeless. And my brother always tried to go play baseball instead of doing his homework.

Every summer the family used to go away to a lake in Canada for a couple of weeks. We had a big, old cottage with a fireplace, but no TV. We would go fishing and swimming every day, and sailing as well. We had great times.

Unit 8, Part 5.

GRANDCHILD:	Happy 90th birthday, Grandma!
GRANDMOTHER:	Oh, thank you, honey.
GRANDCHILD:	How many grandchildren do you have now?
GRANDMOTHER:	Well, the last time I counted there were 21 grandchildren and two great-grandchildren.
GRANDCHILD:	Wow! Can you remember all our names?
GRANDMOTHER:	No, I can't anymore, especially 'cause you live all over the world.
GRANDCHILD:	Yeah, I'm in California and my brother Steve's up in Alaska—he's working for an oil company now, you know.
GRANDMOTHER:	And your Uncle Jim's daughter got married to a Frenchman, so she's in France now.
GRANDCHILD:	And John's company just sent him to Japan!
GRANDMOTHER:	I can't keep up with all of you.
GRANDCHILD:	Well, we can't always keep up with you. You're always going some place.
GRANDMOTHER:	Well, there are still lots of interesting things to do and places to go see . . .
GRANDCHILD:	Oh, I know . . . Where are you going to go next?
GRANDMOTHER:	Well, I've never been to Japan . . . and John *is* living there now . . .

Unit 9, Part 2.

There was an article I read the other day in the newspaper about how people learn things. For example, some people can learn a foreign language just by hearing it, and then trying to speak it. Others have to read it and write it in order to learn it. So some people use their ears more, and others use their eyes to learn new things.

As for me, I can't learn how to use a word processor, for example, just by reading the instruction manual. I have to have someone show me, and then I have to try myself, with the other person to help if I get something wrong. That's how I've learned a lot of things, like repairing my bicycle and using my personal computer. Those are all mechanical things, skills.

But with other more abstract subjects, such as economics or psychology, it helps me a lot if I can talk about or write about what I read or heard in a lecture. I have to do something in order to learn and remember what I learned. I guess that's true for most people.

Unit 9, Part 6.

RECEPTIONIST: Good morning, New Age Dance School. Can I help you?

CALLER: Yes, I'm interested in taking lessons in ballroom dancing.

RECEPTIONIST: OK—have you taken dance lessons before?

CALLER: Well, when I was a kid I studied ballet for a few years, but nothing since then.

RECEPTIONIST: OK. So you're interested in ballroom or social dancing.

CALLER: Yeah . . . you know, fox trot, waltz, samba . . .

RECEPTIONIST: How often do you want to take lessons? Once a week, twice a week?

CALLER: Once a week sounds about right. I don't have a lot of free time. You do have evening classes, don't you?

RECEPTIONIST: Yes, we have classes on Monday and Thursday evenings from 6 to 8 o'clock.

CALLER: Thursday evenings would be good for me, but 6 o'clock is a little early.

RECEPTIONIST: Well, we also have a class from 7 to 9.

CALLER: That sounds better. What do I have to do to enroll?

RECEPTIONIST: Why don't you come down to the school? Our address is . . .

Unit 10, Part 2.

GAIL: There's so much traffic nowadays . . . people are always rushing some place. And the pollution . . .

JOAN: Yeah . . . sometimes old-fashioned ways are better . . . less stress and all.

GAIL: I read in the newspaper the other day about people commuting to work by bicycle in London and New York.

JOAN: Well, that's what people used to do.

GAIL: And still do in China.

JOAN: Yes . . . I kind of like slower forms of travel.

GAIL: When I was very young, I crossed the Atlantic from New York to France by ship, on the *Queen Mary*.

JOAN: That must have been wonderful.

GAIL: It certainly was. It took five days. I'll never forget it.

JOAN: I can remember how we children used to wash the dishes after supper every night. Now everyone has a dish washer.

GAIL: And kids these days all have calculators to do their math homework.

JOAN: I could easily give up cars, planes . . . microwave ovens.

GAIL: But I wouldn't want to give up my word processor. Without it, I can't type even one sentence correctly!

Unit 10, Part 5.

One of the most important places for me when I was a child was the public library. We didn't have a big house and so there was no good place to read quietly. There was always someone else around—my parents and brothers and sisters. And I loved to read—novels, plays, history books. So the library was a great place; it had all kinds of books and it was quiet. I used to go there often, at least once a week, to get books, and sometimes to stay and read. The librarians all knew me. I always won the contests they had for reading the most books during the summer vacation.

The library building itself was very nice. It was big and old, with wooden tables and chairs and bookshelves. It was surrounded by trees, and there was a bus stop right nearby so I could easily go there by myself. My parents never complained when I asked to go to the library!

Unit 11, Part 2.

SCOTT: Hi, Sumiko, I heard you went to Bali for ten days.
SUMIKO: Yes, we had a great time.
SCOTT: Where did you go?
SUMIKO: We went to Legian. It's quieter and not so full of tourists as some of the other beaches.
SCOTT: Who did you go with, if I may ask?
SUMIKO: My sister and two girlfriends from work.
SCOTT: So did you just sit around on the beach?
SUMIKO: Well, an hour or so every day. But we did other things too. Bali's a really interesting place. We took local buses and traveled around the island.
SCOTT: Oh, you can do that?
SUMIKO: Sure. It takes time, but we got to see some beautiful temples. And a place where they weave special Balinese cloth.
SCOTT: Did you see any Balinese dancing?
SUMIKO: Yes. It was so fascinating and beautiful. And the music is so exotic.
SCOTT: And the food?
SUMIKO: Good. We had avocado juice and salad made with peanut sauce!

Unit 11, Part 6.

The first time you go to a country where you don't know the language, where the culture is completely different, it's a shock. Suddenly you can't read anything or understand anything. You're hungry and finally find a restaurant that looks OK. But you can't read the menu and so you just point to something. If you're lucky, it's good. You go into a bank to exchange money and it all looks strange. It won't fit into your wallet and it's difficult to remember how much it's worth.

At the hotel, you try to ask the desk clerk some questions, but he can't speak your language very well. The train station has many, many windows and long lines of people waiting. But you can't understand where to go to buy a ticket. So you give up and go to an outdoor restaurant to have something to drink. But the waiter won't come to your table. You didn't know you have to buy a ticket first!

But still, I wouldn't give up traveling. In spite of all the difficulties, it's really exciting seeing new places, tasting new food, and meeting different people.

Unit 12, Part 2.

CARL: Dan, hey, how are you?

DAN: Oh, hi, Carl—well, not very well recently.

CARL: Why? What's wrong? Been having too much fun?

DAN: No . . . overwork, I guess. I've had to do a lot of overtime work and there's a lot of pressure at work right now . . . we're expanding our business overseas.

CARL: So, lots of stress. Modern life is not good for us.

DAN: Exactly! Sometimes I feel I only use the muscles in my head.

CARL: Yeah, I know what you mean. That's too bad. You need exercise. How about some tennis on Sunday?

DAN: Well, Sunday, I have a wedding to go to . . . a colleague of mine from my office is getting married.

CARL: Are you still jogging?

DAN: Yeah, I try to. At least that I can do on my own, anytime.

CARL: Well, I prefer to go work out at the gym instead . . . more interesting.

DAN: Maybe . . . when I can, I go swimming, but the place I usually go to is closed for repair work.

CARL: Well, come with me one evening. You can come as my guest and if you like it you can join my gym. It's a real nice place.

DAN: OK . . . yeah, why not? How about Wednesday after work?

Unit 12, Part 5.

PATRICK: Hey, Matthew, I didn't know you smoked!

MATTHEW: Well, I wish I didn't.

PATRICK: Well, why *do* you?

MATTHEW: I guess I like it. It relaxes me, makes me feel comfortable. Haven't you ever smoked?

PATRICK: I started smoking in high school, but then I made the swimming team.

MATTHEW: And the coach stopped you from smoking?

PATRICK: No. I just decided myself that I wanted to be a good swimmer more than I wanted to smoke.

MATTHEW: So you gave it up.

PATRICK: Right—for good. Why don't you?

MATTHEW: Well . . . I've tried.

PATRICK: You think smoking makes you look more "macho?"

MATTHEW: When I was a teenager, yeah, I guess I did. I thought I looked tough and sophisticated, like James Dean.

PATRICK: And now?

MATTHEW: Of course not. But I'm hooked.

PATRICK: But, hey, you can't let a little thing like a cigarette beat you!

MATTHEW: Yeah . . . and my girlfriend is saying she doesn't want to go out with me anymore if I don't stop, so . . .

Unit 13, Part 2.

REPORTER: Hello, I'm from WNYC. We're interviewing people about their favorite forms of entertainment. Can you tell us what you like to do in your free time?

PERSON 1: Me? Oh, I love to go dancing. I *love* discos, all discos. I usually go at around 11 o'clock and stay all night.

REPORTER: Why do you love discos?

PERSON 1: Oh, the music, the people, the clothes, you know.

REPORTER: And you, what's *your* favorite form of entertainment?

PERSON 2: I like to go to classical music concerts; in particular, I like Beethoven. But I hate modern music.

REPORTER: All modern music? Even jazz?

PERSON 2: Yes, all modern music.

REPORTER: Excuse me, what's your favorite kind of entertainment?

PERSON 3: Movies—though I don't like horror movies or sci-fi movies very much.

REPORTER: How often do you go to the movies?

PERSON 3: At least once a week. I try to go to the second-run theaters. They're cheaper.

REPORTER: Why do you like movies so much?

PERSON 3: I guess because I always dreamed of becoming an actress when I was young.

Unit 13, Part 5.

LINDA: OK, fine, Susan . . . that's great. So see you next Saturday at five in front of the theater . . . Bye.

. . .

Telephones are very useful and very necessary, but sometimes I wish I didn't have one. My life would be a lot more peaceful.

PAM: Yes . . . and televisions. What a waste of time!

LINDA: I like to do things with my hands, creative things, in my free time: sewing, cooking, making bread, knitting. But somehow I never seem to get around to them these days. Either I spend the whole evening on the phone or I'm so tired I just sit in front of the TV.

PAM: You should take up mountain climbing or hiking. There are no telephones or televisions on a hike.

LINDA: You do a lot of hiking, don't you?

PAM: Yes. I belong to a club. We usually go somewhere twice a month for the day.

LINDA: That's a good idea. So you always have a group of people to hike with.

PAM: Exactly. But I'm also involved in an environmental organization. We have study groups and we give talks at PTA meetings and to children.

LINDA: Hmm . . . that sounds interesting.

PAM: Well, why don't you come along? The next meeting is next Tuesday.

Unit 14, Part 2.

ANDY: Hey, Pitak, if you had lots of money and time, where would you like to travel?

PITAK: Me? I'd like to be one of the first people to travel in space, to the moon maybe.

SUE LING: What? Why do you want to do that?

ANDY: I wouldn't want to do that at all. I plan to travel around the world, our world. How about you, Sue Ling?

SUE LING: Well, I don't know, Andy . . . I've only seen the States so far.

PITAK: But think of it, the moon. The earth would be so boring, Andy!

ANDY: Boring . . . ? I haven't seen the blue Mediterranean yet or the temples in India . . . or the Great Wall in China.

PITAK: Well, that's true . . . I want to see the Himalayas, Nepal.

ANDY: But I also want to *do* something, you know, help other people here on our earth.

PITAK: Well, you're studying pre-med, right?

ANDY: Right. So I'm thinking of going to Africa for a couple of years after I finish medical school.

SUE LING: Hmm . . . I'm hoping to go to the Philippines. My degree in agricultural technology may be useful . . . and I'd learn a lot by working there.

PITAK: I guess I'd like to go live in Japan for a few years—learn the language and get some experience working in a Japanese company.

ANDY: That's not a bad idea.

PITAK: Then I'll go back to Thailand and do what I can to help my country.

SUE LING: Hey, I know—let's all promise that, ten years from now, we'll all meet some place and have a reunion.

ANDY: Yeah, and see if any of our dreams have come true.

U n i t   1 4 ,   P a r t   5 .

TINA: Hey, Marty, it's the end of the year. Exams will soon be over. Let's have a party before we all leave for the summer.

MARTY: Great idea, Tina! What do you think, Bob?

BOB: Well . . . [*sounding reluctant*]

TINA: Oh, come on! It can be a real pot luck, so we don't have to prepare a lot of food.

MARTY: Yeah. All we have to do is clean up this apartment a little . . .

TINA: And Sheila and I can help . . .

BOB: OK, OK, Tina! I'll take care of the music.

TINA: Great! Now, when should we have it?

MARTY: How about the last night, after the exams are all over. Friday the 15th?

TINA: Fine . . . and who should we invite?

BOB: Don't invite Mike. He broke my stereo the last time he was here.

TINA: Oh, come on. He's OK. He didn't mean to.

MARTY: Let's invite the women across the street—Yuki, Iris Chen, and Wu Yi An.

TINA: And José. Maybe he'll bring his guitar and sing Mexican songs for us.

BOB: Can I invite Kristina?

MARTY: [*whispers*] Oh, that's his new girl friend . . . [*out loud*] . . . Not if your old girlfriend's coming . . .

Answer Key

Unit 1

1A 1B   2A   3D   4C

2A 2

2B *Kinds of work:* Carrying the bread and rolls and cakes through into the store and putting them on the shelves; cashier

Good/bad points: Smell of fresh-baked bread and cakes (good); Not difficult (good); Sometimes the store is full and people push (bad); She doesn't earn a lot of money (bad)

Days: Monday, Thursday, Saturday

Hours: All day Saturday; 3–7 Monday and Thursday

Pay: Not very good

4A 1T   2T   3F   4T

4B stores two crowded/unexciting clothes/impossible to find something one likes

4C 1   to buy good clothes for me
     2   attractive
     3   your helping me

Unit 2

2A 1T   2F   3T   4T
     5T

2B skiing /ski jumping /hang-gliding

2C *Past:* climbing trees, riding his bicycle really fast, badminton

Present: skiing, ski jumping, football

Future: hang-gliding, mountain climbing

4A on a badminton court: shuttlecock, racket, net
on a baseball field: ball, bat
on a golf course: ball, club, hole
on a tennis court: ball, racket, net

4B golf

5A 1T   2T   3F   4T

5B *Plus:* good shoes, proper clothing
Minus: a special place, special equipment, a partner, a special time

5C *Plus:* do warm-up exercises, jog for a short time at first
Minus: jog every day, eat just before or after you jog, have a cold drink just after you jog

Unit 3

1A 1B   2C   3D   4A

2A 1F   2T   3F   4T
     5F

2B studio/balcony/bath/kitchen

2C fish, salads, fruit

3A 1   In an apartment near the park.
     2   It has two rooms.
     3   Yes, of course.
     4   The living room is, but the bedroom's pretty small. But it's OK.
     5   Mm, no . . . it's pretty cheap.
     6   Yes, I am—but it isn't perfect, you know.
     7   Well, there's a lot of traffic on the street outside—so it's a little noisy.
     8   No, it's also a little cold—the heating system isn't very good.
     9   I'd like to have a small house near the ocean—with an orange tree in the yard.

5A 1 yes   2 yes   3 no   4 yes
     5 yes.

5B bed, bookcases, stereo, TV, stove

Unit 4

1A 1B   2C   3E   4A
     5D   6F

1B (answers will vary)

3A 1F   2T   3F   4T
     5F   6F

3B *Past:* she's been a swimmer since she was six; on the swimming team of her high school; part-time jobs—baby-sitting, delivering newspapers, clerical work, tutoring

Now: volunteer swimming instructor for handicapped children

Future: wants to go to Spain next year to study Spanish

4A Can you speak French or Spanish?
Can you type? Can you drive?
Who was your last employer?
What was your last job?
Can you start next Monday?
How many people does the hotel employ?
Will I sometimes have to work at night?
How many hours a week will I have to work?
How many days off will I have?
What will my salary be?

5A 1   no/I don't know (students' answers may vary)
     2   no/I don't know (students' answers may vary)
     3   yes
     4   yes

5B flying overseas, going to different places, beautiful sights, discounts on hotels and flights

5C annoying passengers

Unit 5

1A 1D 2A 3C 4B

2A *The food:* interesting, awful, over-cooked, excellent

The service: slow, friendly, unfriendly, fast

The inside of the restaurant: attractive, modern, elegant, shabby

3A 2

3B *Negative:* service, food, inside of restaurant

Positive: dessert

3C 1d 2f 3e 4b
5a 6c

6A 1 get everything ready
2 cook the noodles
3 cook the ground meat
4 chop the parsley
5 slice the mozzarella cheese
6 fill the baking dish
7 bake it in the oven
8 let it stand for ten minutes

6B Now, in the <u>top</u> (bottom) of the baking dish, put a <u>thick</u> (thin) layer of the tomato sauce. Then put down a layer of <u>cheese</u> (lasagna noodles). Sprinkle some of the ground meat over the <u>cheese</u> (noodles). Put some ricotta cheese on the meat and then slices of the <u>ricotta</u> (mozzarella) cheese here and there over the meat as well. Finally, sprinkle some Parmesan cheese and a little chopped <u>onion</u> (parsley) all over it.

Unit 6

2A 1 (answers will vary)
2 He also gets money from his parents.

2B CDs, cassettes, movies, going out, travel

5A 1 coins   2 check   3 bill
4 credit card
1 coins and bill
(other answers will vary)

5B 1d   2h   3e   4b
5a   6f   7g   8c

6A 1

6B 1 no   2 yes   3 yes   4 no
5 yes

Unit 7

2A No, she isn't.

2B practical, comfortable, easy to take care of

2C monotony

5A 1

5B 1F   2T   3T   4T
5T

6A *Hair:* 1—short and curly; 2— shoulder-length and wavy; 3—long and straight

Face: 1—round; 2—oval; 3— square

Some other useful words: 1— glasses; 2—beard; 3— moustache

7 2 short
3 light
4 old-fashioned
5 special
6 formal
7 cheap

Unit 8

2A *summer vacation:* 3
fighting with her brother: 2
chores at home: 1

2B 1T   2T   3T   4F
5T   6T

2C 1 Washing the dishes and taking care of the pets.
2 Baseball, fishing, swimming, and sailing.

4 *Female:* daughter-in-law, sister-in-law, wife, grandmother, cousin, granddaughter, mother, daughter, niece, mother-in-law, aunt, sister, stepmother

Male: brother, cousin, grandfather, uncle, father-in-law, son-in-law, grandson, son, brother-in-law, husband, stepfather, nephew, father

5A 1F   2T   3F   4T
5T

5B France, Alaska, California, Japan

5C Possible sentences (answers will vary):
1 There are two main topics in the conversation: grandchildren and travel.
2 One reason the grandmother can't remember the names of her grandchildren and great-grandchildren is because there are so many of them.
3 The grandmother is very active. She wants to go to Japan.

Unit 9

2A *learning a language:* 1
learning a skill: 2
learning abstract subjects: 3
2B *Skills:* using a word processor,
using a computer, repairing
a bicycle
abstract subjects: psychology,
economics
2C 1 yes   2 no   3 yes   4 no
5 yes   6 yes   7 yes
3 1 history
2 Spanish
3 physics
4 music
5 English
6 mathematics
7 typing
8 chemistry
6A IT   2F   3F   4T
6B ballroom/waltz/Thursday/
six/better

Unit 10

2A 3
2B bicycles, ships, dish washers,
calculators, cars, planes,
microwave ovens, word
processors
2C word processor
3 1 a refrigerator
2 (an airplane)
3 an electric lightbulb
4 a watch
5 a telephone
6 a television
7 a ballpoint pen
8 a paperback
9 a washing machine
10 a calculator
11 a photocopier
12 a car
5A 1, 2, 3, 4
5B Possible sentences (answers
will vary):
1 She lived in a small house.
2 She went to the library at
least once a week.
3 Yes, they did.
4 It was big and old.

Unit 11

2A 1 Two people are talking.
2 Yes, they are.
3 Four people went to Bali.
4 No, they don't. (Three
people work together.)
2B Possible sentences:
1 They sat on the beach.
2 They traveled around the
island.
3 They saw Balinese
dancing.
4 They had avocado juice and
salad made with peanut
sauce.
2C temples, cloth, dancing, music
4A 1 restaurant
2 bar
3 swimming pool
4 sauna
5 tennis courts
6 golf course
7 fishing
8 riding
9 pets welcome
10 facilities for disabled
people
11 parking lot
12 conference room
13 children welcome
14 laundry service
6A 1T   2T   3T   4F
5F
6B you can't read anything or
understand anything; it's
difficult to order food in
restaurants; the money looks
strange and it's difficult to
remember how much it's
worth; the desk clerks in
hotels can't speak your
language very well; at train
stations you don't know where
to go to buy a ticket

Unit 12

1B Possible sentences:
You shouldn't smoke.
You shouldn't drink too much
coffee.
You shouldn't eat too much.
You shouldn't work too hard.
You shouldn't lie in the sun all
day long.
2A 1 Two men are talking. They
are friends.
2 The topic of their
conversation is stress.
2B 1 Possible answer: He has
been working too hard and
he has not been exercising.
2C 1 a, d
2 b, c
2B Yes, he does succeed. At the
end of the conversation they
agree to go to the gym on
Wednesday after work.
5A He is trying to persuade his
friend to stop smoking.
(Students' answers to the
second part of the question
will vary.)
5B 1F   2T   3T   4F
5T
5C 1 So you gave it up.
2 Right—for good. Why don't
you?
3 Well . . . I've tried.
4 You think smoking makes
you look more "macho?"
5 When I was a teenager,
yeah, I guess I did.

Unit 13

2A discos, classical music concerts, horror movies

2B three

Speaker 1: a young man, probably in his twenties

Speaker 2: an older man, well-educated

Speaker 3: a young career woman

2C "I guess because I always dreamed of becoming an actress when I was young."

4A
1 listening to music
2 arranging flowers
3 taking photographs
4 reading
5 visiting museums
6 working in the garden
7 parachuting
8 collecting stamps
9 climbing
10 playing the piano

5A Two people are talking. They are probably friends.

5B Plus: sewing, cooking, knitting, hiking

Minus: telephones, televisions

5C
1 One of the women likes to do things with her hands, creative things: for example, sewing, cooking, making bread, knitting.

2 The other woman is involved in two groups: a hiking group and an environmental group.

3 The second group gives talks at PTA meetings and to children.

Unit 14

2A 1

2B 1c 2a 3b

2C
1 — the Mediterranean
2 — India
3 — China
4 — the Himalayas
5 — Nepal
6 — Africa
7 — the Philippines
8 — Japan

5A
1 Agree
2 Agree
3 Disagree (it'll be pot luck)
4 Agree
5 Agree
6 Disagree (he sings Mexican songs)
7 Agree

5B 1c 2d 3e 4a
5b

Longman Group UK Limited,
Longman House, Burnt Mill, Harlow,
Essex CM20 2JE, England
and Associated Companies throughout the world.

First published 1990
Third impression 1992

Set in Linotron 300 11/14 Century

Printed in Hong Kong
AP/03

ISBN 0 582 05147 9

Acknowledgements
We are grateful to the following for permission to reproduce photographic material in this book:

AGE FOTO Stock for page 32 (top right); Barnabys Picture Library for pages 8 (top left) and 16 (top); Camera Press Limited for page 32 (top left); Dillons The Bookstore for pages 64 and 73; Greg Evans Photo Library for pages 16 (bottom right) and 24 (bottom left); Robert Harding Picture Library for pages 8 (bottom left) and 16 (bottom left); Longman Photographic Unit for pages 22, 24 (bottom right) and 59; Network Photographers for page 24 (top left); Our Price Records for page 8 (top right); Tony Stone Photo Library – London for pages 8 (bottom right), 24 (top right) and 32 (bottom).